Muslim Portraits

Muslim Portraits
Everyday Lives in India

Edited by
Mukulika Banerjee

Indiana University Press
Bloomington & Indianapolis

This book is a publication of

Indiana University Press
601 North Morton Street
Bloomington, Indiana 47404-3797 USA

www.iupress.indiana.edu

Telephone orders   800-842-6796
Fax orders   812-855-7931
Orders by e-mail   iuporder@indiana.edu

First published in 2008 by YODA PRESS
© 2008 by Mukulika Banerjee

Manufactured in India

Cataloging information is available from the Library of Congress.

ISBN 978-0-253-35341-2 (cl)
ISBN 978-0-253-22098-1 (pbk)
1 2 3 4 5 14 13 12 11 10 09

In Memoriam

Aparna Rao (1950–2005)
friend and colleague

Contents

Acknowledgments

M y first thanks are to the contributors of this volume. It was the
enthusiasm with which they greeted my unusual request for individual
portraits rather than academic papers that made this volume possible.
Each one of them responded immediately with a suggestion and a story of
the person they would choose to profile almost as if they had anticipated
my request. Rather than complain about my editorial demands for more
literary-style essays, they insisted that this kind of writing though hard,
was fulfilling and enjoyable and helped them share the stories and
observations which otherwise remained neglected in their academic
writings. This made my job of demanding revisions much easier and
made the volume genuinely collaborative.

The relatively young Yoda Press, led by the admirable Arpita Das, made
it possible for the book to be published. While more established publishers
hesitated about publishing this volume, Arpita was encouraging and believed
in the book as soon as she had read it. I would like to express my heartfelt
thanks to her and her colleagues for their efficient handling of this book.
Rebecca Tolen at Indiana University Press was similarly encouraging and it
gives me great pleasure to entrust them with the global distribution of this
volume. Warm thanks also to friend and collaborator Oroon Das, who as
always produced a fine and unusual cover design for the book.

My thanks also go to The Leverhulme Trust and University College
London for funding a period of sabbatical when this volume was put
together. The British Academy funded my previous research on *The Sari*,
during which a number of ideas in this book emerged. The Nuffield
Foundation and DFID have funded my ongoing research on popular
perceptions of democracy in India, and this gave me the chance to live and

work in two Muslim villages in the Indian state of West Bengal. I would like to thank all these funding bodies for their generous financial support.

I thank all the people of 'Madanpur' and 'Chishti' for sharing with me their lives and ideas for over a decade. It is their everyday practices of being Muslim, of celebrating festivals, innumerable discussions based on the Bengali translations of the Qur'an, patient explanations about how they do things and what they think and believe, that has given me much of my understanding about lived Islam. The luxury of the wide-ranging conversations I had with them made it possible to raise the questions I could never ask while living in Pashtun society before, when the urgency of doing fieldwork in the North West Frontier Province of Pakistan as an Indian citizen made it imperative to only focus on specific research issues I had at that time. Still, the experience of living, of keeping *roza* and celebrating Id, of regulating daily life by prayer, of sharing food and learning the manners in both these contexts, the Pashtun and the Bengali, provided a varied sense of South Asian Islam.

My colleagues in the UK, India and elsewhere have been excellent interlocutors in making sense of fieldwork. The writings of several scholars have provided both education and inspiration. I am particularly appreciative of the insights shared by Shahid Amin, Richard Eaton, Mushir-ul-Hasan, Murray Last, T.N. Madan, Danny Miller, Yogi Sikand and Jit Uberoi in conversations and writings over the years.

And as always, I thank my family who have shaped this book in their own ways. My parents made our home a thoroughly cosmopolitan space without ever posturing to do so. My father's years at Loknarayan Jai Prakash (Irwin) Hospital meant we were always the beneficiaries of Id goodies from an endless stream of grateful Muslim patients from Turkman Gate in Old Delhi. Through many salutations, conversations, and my father's stories, we grew up knowing the worlds of car mechanics, tailors and fishmongers who made up the vibrant commercial life of Shahjahanabad. My mother did not think it the slightest bit ironical to regulate our disciplined Bengali middle class life by the *azan* that called worshippers to prayer from the mosque located behind our house. Indeed, we were used to waking up to the first *azan* on dark winter mornings to prepare for exams or dreading the last *azan* that marked the curfew to come indoors from games of badminton and *pithoo* in fading light. It was routine in our household to light the evening lamp and blow the conch shell in that thoroughly Bengali dusk ritual once the penultimate *azan* of the day had been called. Our only neighbors were a gentle couple who kept to themselves, but with whom we never failed to exchange greetings and delicacies on our respective festivals. It was only in my teens that I realized that the quiet gentlemen who delivered the delicious *sevai* his wife had prepared was Dr. Ahmed Ali, the Principal of Zakir Hussain College. When I later set my heart on traveling to the North West Frontier for doctoral research, he enthusiastically responded to my desire to learn the Urdu script by finding me an excellent Persian teacher. All these and more no doubt shaped the habitus that engendered my interest in Muslim societies. I thank my sisters for our shared ideas and sensibilities that gave shape to much of my academic interest in Muslim societies. For this book, I would also like to record special thanks to my younger sister Krittika, who unfailingly responded to every draft that I sent her. For me, she exemplified the reader I had in mind, of the reader outside of academia that I wanted all the essays in this volume to reach out to. Each of her comments, uncompromising but always encouraging, was invaluable. Special thanks also to my brother-in-law, Yogendra Yadav for sharing with me the extraordinary story of his naming and for his permission to use it here. It was my husband Julian Watts who reminded me that of all my stories this was the one to share in the context of this volume. I thank him for being not only a tolerant but keen listener. It has been in the narratives that I have constructed for him to describe India that I have come to realize the significance of much that I took for granted as a child. My final thanks are to my daughter Aria Gitanjali who provided me constant company as she took shape herself while this book was conceived, edited and put into place. I hope that she will enjoy reading these wonderful portraits one day.

Introduction

MUKULIKA BANERJEE

In September 1963, a baby boy, the third child after two girls, was born to Hindu parents in a north Indian town. He was named Parvez. The choice of a Muslim name for a valued son was unusual, and in this case it was not dictated by fashion, a favorite film star or gratitude to a saint as often happens in families. So why was a Muslim name chosen by Hindu parents? For an answer, we need to return to events nearly 25 years before Parvez's birth.

Parvez's grandfather was the Warden of a Government Boys School where both Hindu and Muslims studied. Parvez's father, the son of the Warden, also studied at that school and enjoyed the privileges of the other children, living as they all did on campus with plenty of time to spend in each other's company as they played, ate and studied together. It was the secure, contented existence of a well-run institution in a small mofussil town in colonial India. However, on a cold February morning in 1938 this calm was shattered. It was the day of the festival of Id and as the Muslims congregated in large numbers for prayers, a provocation turned the gathering violent. As the violence grew into rioting, a group of Muslim men arrived at the Boys School and demanded to see the Warden. As he emerged to face the rioters, he was ordered to hand over all the Hindu students to the impatient mob. The Warden refused. He was reminded that as a Hindu himself, his life might be spared if he handed over his students. But the Warden insisted that he was responsible for his wards and that looking after their welfare was his first priority. The mob had no patience for such explanations and murdered him right there, in the school, within sight of the students and other staff, as they chopped his head off with a *gandasa*. His 9-year-old son who had been hidden away with his mother was mercifully spared the sight.

Ten years later, the same young boy witnessed violence in the wake of Partition. This time, Hindus did the killing and large numbers of Muslims were massacred. But it was the same violence, perpetrated in the name of religion, the violence that had snatched his father away in a moment and changed his life forever. An idyllic existence and excellent education had given way to a return to the native village and its inferior school, his mother's refusal to depend on relatives which made their life hard and the loss of his friends. As the young man shaped his life through these years, 'forgetting' the traumatic memories of his childhood and trying to make sense of the violence of his youth, he read, thought, and educated himself in history and politics. By the time he married in 1952 as a young lecturer in Economics, he made one resolution for himself. He would give his children Muslim names. The popular lyrics of the film song—*Na Hindu banega na Mussalman banega, insaan ki aulad hai insan banega* (the child of a human shall be human, not a Hindu nor a Muslim)—perfectly represented his thoughts and the individual's revulsion of a divisive, violent communal ideology.

Accordingly, when their first child was born five years later, his wife and he named her Nazneen. But this provoked hysterical and horrified advice from well-meaning friends around them. A Hindu girl with such a name would never find a Hindu groom, they warned. After much soul-searching, the couple reluctantly agreed to hold off their decision until they had a son. Their next child was also a girl who was given a Hindu name for the same reasons. And then, having waited over 10 years after making their decision, the couple could finally put their ideas into practice. They named their son Parvez. But while the risk forecast for the girls had been for the future, trouble started for Parvez right from nursery school. His friends began to tease him and ridiculed the idea that a Hindu boy could have a Muslim name and repeatedly asked him if he was secretly a Muslim. Living as they did in an Indian town on the border with Pakistan where no Muslim inhabitants remained, the young Parvez had no idea who a 'Muslim' was. His father, when faced with this innocent question, took the boy to visit the town's local mosque. But this was no Taj Mahal to impress a young child with. The derelict mosque looked like a haunted house, empty, abandoned by worshippers who had been either killed or had fled across the border two decades ago. Its silent presence stood as testimony of past violence and for a child it looked scary and daunting. At school meanwhile, the teasing got even more unbearable as classmates began to question Parvez's legitimacy and asked if he was really his parents' child? If so, why would Hindu parents distance themselves from their child by naming him after a Muslim, they wondered. For a 4-year-old this proved to be the final straw. He was the only one in school who was continuously teased about his name and so one day, the young Parvez gave his parents an ultimatum 'Change my name or I don't go to school'. Unwilling to traumatize the young child for the sake of his beliefs, the father picked three Hindu names, wrote them down on pieces of paper and asked Parvez to choose one in a lottery. He picked 'Amitabh' and that became his formal name from that day. The playground teasing stopped immediately as the children felt strangely reassured now that their Hindu friend had finally been given a Hindu name. The irony was that after this tortured path to its adoption, no one actually ever bothered to use the name 'Amitabh' which was promptly elevated to the formal, the distant and the official world of certificates and bank statements. Neighbors, teachers and friends continued to use the name 'Parvez' and it was as if its new informal status allowed its use without aggravation.

While Parvez's story dates to an earlier India, it would probably be the same today. A Hindu boy called Parvez in twenty-first-century India would probably face the same social cacophony of advice, censure and teasing as Parvez and his parents did in the 1950s and 1960s. His story provokes us to confront the social conventions of naming which dictate that children of Hindu parents should be given Hindu names and Muslim children Islamic ones. In a society in which surnames provide a ready reckoning of caste and religion, first names too are expected to locate a person firmly in a specific category. Together the two (or more) names of any individual are expected to reflect without ambiguity, the gender, caste and religion of that individual. We may ask why this is of such importance despite such a long shared history of the two communities in a single country. To a certain extent, naming is an essential boundary maintenance device which most communities of the world utilize to maintain the exclusivity of their group. But as Parvez's story reveals, in India, it is clearly more than just that. The vociferous teasing and opprobrium faced by Parvez's family revealed that the transgression of Hindu and Muslim identities in any way, however minor, was unacceptable. People were clearly not willing to be forced to use a Muslim name to refer to a Hindu child for the fear of pollution, as if the very name could eddy the purity of a child's religious identity. But as we can reasonably conclude, Parvez's father's decision to give his children Muslim names in the first place, stemmed from a comparable fear, if far more personal. He had probably realized how easy it could be for him to see all Muslims as 'the enemy' as a result of his personal tragedy of losing his father to some Muslim rioters. His decision to give his children Muslim names would force him on the other hand to use these names with love rather than with hate which he had every justifiable right to. And given that all parents have room for creativity in the choosing of first names of their children he had exercised this prerogative. What he hadn't anticipated was how his creativity was circumscribed by aesthetic rather than any political or ethical criteria.[1] Ultimately therefore he had to give in to the social pressure of keeping his child's Hindu identity unambiguous and the absent Muslims of his town, alongside all other Muslims in general had to remain nameless and faceless.

And so it is in contemporary India, that for the purpose of most everyday discussions, 'the Muslim' is nameless, probably bearded or veiled, impoverished, fecund, pious and/or militant but rarely with a personal story or biography. It is an identity that is often reduced to a statistic, to make an argument in favour or against the Muslim. Is this because while there exists a rich corpus of historical, demographic, philosophical, political, and even activist writing on Muslims in India, there is not much available that allows us to meet and learn who these people are, where they live, what their opinions are? The obvious cultural complexity of this community, given it resides in a mosaic-like India, is erased in favor of this monolithic category: 'the Muslim'. The fine-grained portraits in this volume are intended to put some flesh on the bones of this rather two-dimensional category of 'the Muslim' that has emerged and is frequently evoked in public debate and discussion. While such a category is used by both liberals and their detractors, its usage often assumes that we know about the people who populate such a category. A recent study exposed a startling misconception in India about Muslims, even among the most educated.[2] For instance, three quarters of the respondents in a national random sample overestimated the number of Muslims in India by twice the real figure, no doubt having fallen prey to the

[1] Naming boys of a certain generation born to Communist supporters in Kerala Stalin or in Bengal Pablo, was not unusual; in north India, naming trends have tended to follow film stars or politicians.

[2] This was the CNN-IBN-*Hindustan Times* State of the Nation survey conducted by the Centre for the Study of Developing Societies in January 2006.

most popular myth of the exponential growth of the Muslim population compared to all other communities. Writing about the Mussulman in India, the historian Shahid Amin has pointed out that 'with stereotypes we leave biography and history behind, recognizing those different from us largely through visible signs, as if such human beings belonged to a different species altogether'. This volume strives towards breaking down, challenging and humanizing this category by presenting a set of portraits of Muslims in contemporary India. In a climate of widespread stereotypes and prejudice this book attempts to offer a chance to read about ordinary and real lives.

Since the destruction of the Babri Masjid at the end of 1992 something changed fundamentally for Muslims in India, and for everyone else too. The riots following December 1992 unleashed a decade in which pogroms against Muslim communities became shamefully regular occurrences and were further compounded by a growing global legitimacy for Islamophobia. One heinous mid-air attack by elusive terrorists in New York in September 2001 sanctioned a multitude of attacks on vulnerable Muslim populations who lived and worked on the ground in many nations. India worsened its record with the orchestrated pogroms in Gujarat in February 2002 during which middle-class Hindus engaged in crimes of looting, rape and murder. As a result, whether or not they were directly in the firing line, being Muslim everywhere in India changed. What had been hitherto implicit and unsaid in some minds, was vocalized freely. The loyalty of Muslims was openly questioned, their very existence in a country where Hindus are a majority was seen as anomalous and they were told quite explicitly by the large Hindu right-wing cadres to 'put up or shut up'. Even for those who lived in India as naturally as any of their neighbors, issues of nationalism, second-class citizenship and personal security became urgent concerns. In this climate, a growing movement of an international Muslim *ummah* backed by financial aid towards providing education and welfare could not be ignored by what is a largely poor Muslim population in India with a large 'developmental deficit'. It is not surprising that the number of Islamic seminaries has grown since 2001, greater emphasis is placed on acquiring the outward symbols of Muslim identity and the suspicion of Hindu activists has escalated. The protagonists of this book all live in this same India in which pogroms of hate, state violence, food insecurity, illiteracy and joblessness have become everyday facts. The individuals described in this book show us how individual Muslims, living in such a milieu, cope. They find avenues for self-improvement, engage in debate and discussion, and above all, utilize the most important facet of being Indian: their franchise. Muslims vote in larger numbers than their other religious counterparts, thereby justly celebrating the one advantage they have over most other Muslims in other parts of the world. As the Sachar Commission report published in November 2006 showed, the use of the fundamental identity of citizenship that is available to all Indians, can transform the discourse of the 'developmental deficit' among Indian Muslims in a way that made it more akin to 'developmental initiatives'.

While no volume can provide a comprehensive picture of the lives of all Muslims in India, the 11 portraits presented here are in many ways 'typical' and certainly 'real' and add something more to what we already know. They aim to introduce the reader to real people and are neither journalistic features nor creative fictions. Instead, these essays are based on the lives of real individuals whom the author has known over a period of years. The authors have each had a long-term research interest in Muslim societies in India and have published about politics, religion, material culture, health, education and other pressing issues in their scholarly publications. But in these essays they profile one single individual whom they have met in the course of their research and whose story they found compelling. The essays they have produced are therefore not a passing journalistic interest in the subject or the result of quick impressions collected during a whistle-stop tour of 'Muslim areas'. The authors included here have voluntarily spent long stretches of time, in some cases over 20 years, in the same areas of India, getting to know generations of families living there, noting the changes from year to year, sharing in the highs and lows of the people who live there and they intend to continue their study long into the future.

While planning such a volume, the 'portrait' format seemed particularly suitable. Portraits of individuals as we know from art, draw the viewer to examine minutiae which offer clues about the subject's life and times. While ruminating on the contours of a person's face in a painting, we wonder about past events and future hopes which put those lines on the face. It is for this reason, that we invited social scientists for whom landscapes are the customary genre to change canvasses to describe not socio-economic issues but particular people. As a result, these writers have portrayed individuals who have normally stood cheek-by-jowl with hundreds of others in a large canvas, but have here focussed attention on them in a separate frame. The landscape remains, but only by suggestion and only as a backdrop to this particular individual's life-story. And as is the case with a painting, a finished portrait is the result of a particular encounter between the artist and his subject. So it is with writers. The questions they asked, their interpretations of the answers, what they observed and concluded, what particular anecdote moved them, the language they used to describe them, are all the result of their personal individual interpretation of their subject's responses. As one joint authored essay in this volume illustrates very clearly, two different people meeting the same person may have very different experiences, resulting in two different 'takes' of the same portrait.

The subjects of this volume live in different parts of India, speak different languages, eat different foods, do various kinds of work, but are all Muslim. India is fairly unique in boasting of a community of Muslims characterized by such diversity. And this diversity lies, as we know, at the very heart of Islam in India. Muslim women in Bengal wear saris and *sindoor*, those in Lakshwadeep have visiting husbands, in Kashmir people found the introduction of greetings in Urdu in the 1990s a strange development, in Bombay Muslims join in Ganesh Chaturthi processions and so on. As Mushirul Hasan recently pointed out—the 'essence of Indian Islam is its mixed tradition'. This diversity has a taken-for-granted quality, a sort of inevitable part of belonging to the Indian mosaic. But what is the virtue of this diversity, we may ask. Is it not just an inevitable consequence of being part of India? Or does it also teach us something about the ability of monotheistic religions to flourish in thoroughly diverse cultural settings. Whether seen historically or spatially, the differences between Muslims across time and space are enormous. To reflect this diversity you will find portraits of people from different regions here. Not all are represented and while obvious places such as Lucknow and Hyderabad feature, unusual ones such as Androth Island and Bhuj do so as well. As a result, no two portraits presented here are alike. The dilemmas faced by a low-caste woman weaver in Tamil Nadu is quite unlike that of a young *madrasah* teacher in Uttar Pradesh. Similarly, the life-world of a young man in Lucknow is quite unlike that of a local don in a Mumbai slum. They are as different as any random group of Indians are likely to be. It so happens that they are also Muslim. By describing individual lives we hope to convey the sheer diversity of what is often glossed over with the homogenizing category of 'the Muslim'. By noting this diversity, any stereotypes we may harbor about what a Muslim is, is likely to be shattered.

This is perhaps most true of one of the most ubiquitous stereotypes of all, 'the mad *mullah*' with his regulation beard angrily issuing *fatwa*s. Brian Didier's essay introduces us to just such a person. By sharing the author's own preconceptions and judgments, we confront our own. His initial fear and reticence with such a taciturn personality, reflects our own inability to see beyond this exterior. Yet, as his interaction with the subject unfolds we discover a man who is more liberal in his attitude to women than his contemporaries, his assessment of a volatile situation is measured and his pride in his region's local Islamic traditions which are increasingly threatened by a universalising dogma is staunch. Aisha, the veiled female *madrasah* teacher from Bijnor is a good example of another popular stereotype. But her biography reveals a different story: behind an all-enveloping *hijab* resides a spirited woman, fluent in several languages, passionate about education, proud of her father who wanted to educate his daughters. But the veil hides this story so well that even her own brother is surprised that she spoke with Patricia Jeffrey at such length. And this makes us wonder whether the veil might in fact be the best way in which Aisha can make herself invisible to get on with her life in a small town in Uttar Pradesh (UP). Many of the women in this book offer such surprises. Like Dr Zakira Ghouse from Hyderabad who at the age of 75 completed her lifelong desire to do a doctorate and this in a city where 84 percent of the women belonging to the 40 percent-strong Muslim population are illiterate. Sylvia Vatuk's long friendship with this woman and her family reveals the many hurdles in the way of such an aspiration, but also the many influences which inspire such dreams. Dr Ghouse's story also points out the crucial role a woman's social class and men can play in supporting women's aspirations when the odds are stacked against them. This observation has been made by academics who have published studies on Muslims women's education. Even though the statistics show that nearly 75 percent of Muslim women in India are illiterate and school enrolment rates continue to be low, 70 percent of Muslim girls from economically better off families attend school whereas only 16.1 percent of poor Muslim girls do.[3] A burning ambition among some women, however, as is in evidence in Soumhya Venkatesh's portrait of a low-caste Tamil Labbi woman Banu Beevi, shows how even the worst circumstances can sometimes be overcome. Despite losing her son to police 'precautionary measures' of locking up young Muslim men at random after a local murder, Banu Beevi enthusiastically embraced every opportunity available to her. She stood for Panchayat elections, applied for National

---

[3] Zoya Hasan and Ritu Menon, 2005, *Educating Muslim Girls: A Comparison of Five Cities*, New Delhi: Kali for Women.

Awards and scraped together funds to travel abroad. In her story, more than any other, one appreciates the importance of political citizenship in a country of deep social inequalities. In Aparna Rao's essay from the highlands of Kashmir, marginal to mainstream India in so many ways, we realize the importance of this citizenship further. Khatija over her 85 years encountered the nation and the state of India in a myriad different ways. But like with rural communities all over the country, the terms 'India' and 'Hindustan' don't signify anything; rather the rest of the country makes itself manifest in their lives through elections, the army, traders and textiles. Rao's essay also shows how the many symbols of Islam which we now take for granted have particular historical trajectories that are erased in their contemporary evocations. Thus we learn that the veil for example, the *burqa*, was introduced to the valley first as a fashionable garment for women bought lovingly by their men as coveted presents from their travels in the plains of India, rather than as a garment of imposed modesty by religious leaders.

That the visibility of being Muslim brings with it an accompanying vulnerability is highlighted through many of the biographies here. For instance in Craig Jeffery's portrait of Zamir we encounter a young man who despite a packed daily schedule makes the time to train in karate because it helps him feel safer 'on the street'. An entrepreneurial young man, he also takes extra tuition in computers to increase his career prospects, which for someone like him are scuppered by the lack of networks or money. Having experienced failure in the 'mainstream' job market, he tries to expand his life chances with training in karate and computers while hoping that his brother will secure a place in the *madrasah* where at least merit counts for more. In a Mumbai neighborhood, visibility is also inextricably linked to envy, as Hansen's portrait of Javeedbhai shows. In this picture of a local 'dada', we are forced to think about the world of this familiar figure. By painting in shades of grey into every aspect of Javeedbhai's biography—his criminal record, his anger, his 'social work', his English-speaking children, Hansen forces us to see beyond what is visible on the surface and to think of circumstances, electoral politics, partisan police forces, and ideals of honor which create such a person.

There has been a lot of debate and much has been written about the coexistence of Muslims and Hindus in India. No story illustrates this better than the portrait of the young man called Islam and his dearest friend, a low-caste Hindu, Jannulal. Ciotti describes the bonds of fictive kinship that these two men have forged between themselves to make their friendship an enduring one. In their everyday lives, they spend as much time together as possible and officiate at each other's rituals, eat their meals together and talk constantly, learning in the process about each other's perspectives on various matters. As a Chamar and as a Muslim, Jannulal and Islam share an understanding of marginality and have formed a fictive bond to cope with their social disadvantages better. Reading about them I was reminded of a poignant remark made by someone in my fieldsite in rural West Bengal. It was believed that just watching men pray at the mosque on special festivals like Id, was itself an act of piety. Accordingly, all Muslim women and low-caste Hindus of the village made it a point to do so. One year as I stood with some Dom friends watching the indistinguishable rows of backs and heads bent in prayer, one elderly woman remarked to me wistfully 'isn't it wonderful Didi, that at least in their religion, all Muslims can pray together. They just learn to stand next to anyone without worrying who it is. Isn't that marvellous?' This important egalitarian spirit among Muslims, however symbolic, clearly has enormous significance for low-caste Hindus and Jannulal is no exception. Through his friendship with his fictive brother, he hopes to experience this spirit vicariously, just as much as Islam learns from the phenomenal enterprise demonstrated by the Chamars in eastern UP. A similar juxtaposition of values is evident in Mayaram's portrait of Abdul, an untouchable, illiterate Muslim who is also a consummate storyteller with a phenomenal memory and love of learning. During the unrest of Partition, while everyone gathered their most precious possessions before going into hiding, Abdul treasured his book, his *'ilm*, his learning, in a baniya's shop. While tossed between the didactic cross currents of belonging and not belonging to different Islamic sects, Abdul continues to tell his stories—of the Mahabharata, of Hazrat Ali, Nabi Rasul and the sacred geography of Rajasthan. In celebration of India's syncretic traditions, most of his stories, regardless of their content, commence with an evocation of the Mirasi's chosen deity, the goddess Bhavani.

All the profiles presented here capture the unexpected contradictions, the hidden surprises in people's lives, which fleeting encounters fail to reveal. MB's story from Bhuj is one such example. Despite the ruination of his comfortable retirement caused by the earthquake, his appetite for broadening his horizons through dictionaries and foreign newspapers remains unabated. In many ways his world proves the credence of globalization. He has pen pals from around the world, speaks with equal passion about Princess Diana's death as he does of his commitment to visiting mosques of all denominations, despite being an Al-Hadith himself. In the essay about him by Simpson and Ibrahim, we learn that long before misfortune put Bhuj on the mental map of Indians, individuals like MB had already encountered the world through books and a multinational religion. A similar sense of discovery infuses Lawrence Cohen's portrait of Z. While on the surface he is like one of thousands of young men trapped in an unwanted marriage, watching Hollywood films for entertainment, suspicious of visiting writers, Cohen paints us a picture that leaves us wondering about what we know. As the story unfolds, the familiarity of such a figure is shaken, as his solemn questions about *visvas* (trust) and friendship raise fundamental issues about who we are, our vain desire to understand other people, the validity of our efforts in even trying to understand the complexities of other people's lives. We invite you to read and enjoy the stories presented here and hope they add some colour to our black and white distinctions, and infuse some doubt into our prejudices while telling real stories about 'the Muslim' in India today.

1

'Islam'
What is in a Name?

MANUELA CIOTTI

I could not talk about Islam, a barber living in a village not far from Varanasi, Uttar Pradesh, without mentioning Jannu Lal, his Hindu friend from an adjacent village. My acquaintance with Islam occurred almost 10 years ago on the occasion of my dinner invitation to Jannu Lal. Dinner was going to take place in a house in the heart of old Varanasi. I had met my friend at an agreed spot in the vegetable bazaar close to the house. I was then told he had also invited Islam, but I could not see him there. Fine, I thought, but a couple of seconds later Jannu Lal informed me that Islam was lost in the bazaar. There was no chance of him finding his way to my house as he had never been there before. And given that the whole market had plunged into darkness as a result of the regular power cuts which 'blessed' the everyday of the holy city, there were not many chances for us to track him down. Nor could we leave Islam to his destiny, Jannu Lal made me understand very clearly. So we embarked on a search which eventually proved to be successful.

That evening the two friends ate together with joy. During our dinner, I realized how dual invitations were an established practice for them. There could not be a feast, festival or a happy occasion where they were not both present. After this episode, I came to know more and more about Islam and his role in the locality where I had been doing my fieldwork. As I will explain below, both Islam's and Jannu Lal's lives have been inextricably linked with and shaped by members of the other's religious community well before they got to know each other and finally became friends. After the dinner episode, I also came to know more about the friendship that bonds Islam and his friend in such a special way. But let me introduce Islam first.

A few kilometres of a *qasba*-like sequence of small shops, businesses and vegetable markets separate Arampur[1], Islam's village, from Varanasi. Islam's family and his community of less than a hundred members have inhabited the village for the last five generations. The majority of the village's inhabitants are Hindu. Islam's *mohalla* is indistinguishable from the countless other *mohalla*s in the area inhabited by low-caste communities. Only the Imam Chauk (on which the *tazia* is placed during Muharram) signals the presence of a Muslim community. There is no mosque in this village so people go for *namaz* to two neighboring villages. Not far from Islam's *mohalla*, there is a burial ground where children gather in the morning to study the Quran under the supervision of the local *maulvi*. Every morning except on Fridays, children learn the Quran for one hour before attending the local primary school a few minutes away from their homes. In the village, communal relations are good: on the occasion of Muharram, both Hindus and Muslims participate in the *tazia* procession, and they share food during Ramadan.

Barber work, sari weaving, and other professions within the informal sector of the economy are the main source of livelihood for Islam's community. Islam, perhaps 50 years old (it is impossible to establish his age), is the head of the Muslim barbers in Arampur. He learnt this profession from his grandfather by being his apprentice for two years. Islam's father had, however, not followed in his father's professional footsteps. A Lala[2] taught Islam's father how to do press work and he had later found a job in a Varanasi press where he had been employed until retirement. Islam, after his apprenticeship with his grandfather and while still unmarried, had moved to Lucknow to live with his *phupha*.[3] There, he would work at his relative's shop and prepare homeopathic medicines. On his return to Arampur three years later, Islam was hired in the same press where his father worked.

At this time, late 1960s–early 1970s, everything seemed to be going on a straight path in Islam's life. He had been working in the press company for four years and had been married to Shezadi, herself from a family of barbers. Her father worked in Mumbai where her brother had opened a barber '*saloon*'. By this time, Shezadi and Islam had also had their first son,

---

[1] A pseudonym.

[2] Local term for a member of the Kayastha community.

[3] Father's sister's husband.

the first of seven children. However, the events which followed reveal how Islam was not satisfied with what he had achieved so far. Without telling anybody in the village, he ran away from his home to Ranchi in Bihar. He was not alone. Sixteen people had decided to embark on this adventure. With the exclusion of his maternal uncle and himself, his fellow runaways were all Hindu and working in the same press. Obviously Islam had planned his escape in absolute secrecy, in consideration of the fact that he was surely not going to obtain permission from his family. Financial motives had persuaded him to leave his village: in Ranchi, he would work in another press but earn considerably more compared to his earnings in Varanasi. In one month, the time it took him to realize that he wanted to return to his home in Arampur, he had made Rs 600, a significant amount back in those days. Around this time, he somehow sensed someone had died in his paternal home. He, therefore, decided to leave Ranchi and upon his arrival at the village, found his intuition had been right. His grandfather had passed away. It was only then that Islam made barber work his permanent source of income.

Not that he had ever considered this choice a bad one. These days, he has no regrets about it and actually emphasizes the financial aspects of being a barber today as compared to being employed in a press. For instance, if he charges Rs 20 for a haircut which only takes a short time to accomplish, he will have to work an entire day to earn the same amount in a press. Islam's father too is happy about his son's decision. If being a barber may be viewed as a matter of concern in terms of status, Islam definitely holds a pragmatic view about this profession. His earnings have increased over the past few years, so the business is good and that is all that matters to him. It is not a coincidence that he has taught the profession to his second son.

His family's barber shops are located on heavily traveled roads—which both crosscut their own village and form its boundaries—for obvious business purposes. These shops are not located in concrete buildings but consist of miniature pile-structures of the type one cannot miss by the roadside in northern India which sell a variety of light goods, ranging from *paan* to disposable shampoo sachets. These tiny boxes standing on four slim legs—made of wood or iron—have three 'built' sides with the front side left open for shopkeepers and customers. And they can be easily locked at night.

Whereas the size of the boxes varies, Islam's is wide and tall enough to contain a chair, a customer and the barber. You can hardly see Islam working at his own shop, however. He cannot be tied down to the shop for more than an hour or two. His love for freedom is too compelling and he likes to roam around and talk with people. As a result, he draws his main income from traveling around as an itinerant barber and has a well-defined area of work within which he journeys. As head of the barber community, he has decided on a geographical division of labor. His area consists of three villages (including Arampur and Jannu Lal's village) and the corresponding market area along the main road.

Sundays are Islam's busiest time, as many people observe a day of rest after a week of work. I can see him in my mind's eye even now walking barefoot carrying his case of instruments and shaving his regular customers or cutting their hair at their homes. A sort of 'at-your-doorstep service'. Alternative bodily postures need to be adopted for shaving and cutting hair if you do not use a chair. I have seen barbers deploying chairs and mirrors without the aid of a fixed shelter, a handy arrangement if one works near one's house so that all the work instruments can be safely stored at night. But these devices are no good if you are a mobile barber. Islam uses a different technique: he squats on the floor in front of his customer (also squatting), and goes about his work. I suppose this is the next best position to the usual one of a sitting customer and a standing barber.

His work does not only include mundane—albeit useful—activities such as shaving his customers and cutting their hair. In the same fashion as Hindu barbers, Islam is also called upon for ritual occasions by many Hindu communities.[4] Sometimes, for example on the occasion of marriages, Islam interacts with Hindu ritual specialists, the local *pandit*s. He enjoys a cordial relationship with them. On these events, before the marriage ceremony takes place Islam collects the items needed for the *puja*, helps the groom to get ready and has the prerogative to place the turban on the latter's head when the *barat* or wedding procession starts from the groom's house and again, when it reaches its final destination.

Generally speaking, Islam's ritual repertoire is the same for all Hindu communities. Where people from any caste may be administered exactly the same rituals, these may vary in length. Within this 'ritual democracy' however, it is the ritual's length which determines Islam's fees. If someone asks for a longer ritual, then she/he will have to pay him extra. As ritual specialist, Islam does not claim any uniqueness to himself. During the marriage

---

[4] Islam however has no ritual role in his own community where the latter as a whole performs ritual activities.

seasons or when unpredictable events like deaths occur, he sometimes cannot manage all the work by himself. Therefore, Islam reserves the right to send his brother to perform rituals on his behalf. Where Islam's business involves interacting with many Hindu communities, he is not an invisible presence amongst them, someone who leaves no trace of his passage. He enjoys such good relations with people that if he is not seen for two or three days and his services are needed, people will send out for him. If he is liked because of his manners, Islam also has his favorite spots within his working area, such as a nearby village he and his wife Shezadi enjoy visiting more than others.

One of the obvious consequences of his ritual activities is that very often he eats out. Where he can easily handle a mobile phone, Islam's engagement with the modern world stops short of eating styles. On the occasion of a lunch invitation made to me by Jannu Lal (and no surprise Islam was there too), Islam explained to me that he does not like the 'buffet system' (he used the English expression). As we were all sitting on the floor of Jannu Lal's mud kitchen eating *puri* and *sabji* off our *thalis*, Islam claimed that if he eats while standing his stomach will not become full. Also, when food is served in a buffet system, it is full of *ghee* and spices which he is not used to. I know he also suffers from diabetes so this might be another factor contributing to his dislike for the rich food served at marriage parties and other events. The modernity of 'helping yourself with the food' is also rejected by Islam on the grounds of his difficulty in multitasking, that is holding a plate, and perhaps a glass, serving himself food and having to eat at the same time while standing.

Islam is not the only worker in the household. His wife Shezadi works too and she travels in the locality to look after her customers, although she does not enjoy traveling as much as her husband does. Like Islam's occupation—although she does not have a ritual role—her business concerns people's aesthetics: she does manicures and pedicures, decorates women's hands and feet with henna, and applies color to their feet on special occasions, in particular, during marriages. Hair-cutting is not included in the range of services Shezadi provides. In villages, women do not have their hair cut and those who do, are the ones who are more affluent and accustomed to visiting beauty parlours located in urban areas. Marriages form Shezadi's largest share of work. She is called upon at these events by the Hindu communities of Arampur and another nearby village. Shezadi has learnt this profession from her mother-in-law who, like Islam, has quite evidently no objection in her engaging in remunerative work. This business is at the center of Shezadi's life and she constantly hopes for more work for herself. And Shezadi is not the only working woman in her community. Nor does she suffer from mobility restrictions as far as work is concerned. As I mentioned earlier, she travels outside her home and also has women seeking her services at her house. Shezadi would have liked to teach this work to her daughters and her daughter-in-law but they are not interested. Like many village women who have gone beyond the early stage of marriage, have had children and have become grandmothers, she shows an assertive persona and does not tolerate those who do not respect her business. And more importantly, those who do not want to give her the due payment for her services. She told me of one time when customers did not want to pay her the agreed fee. She then started a fight, threw things up in the air, and walked away from her customers' house shouting at them '*If you come to my place, I'll give you more [money]!*'.

✱　✱　✱

But how did the friendship between Islam and Jannu Lal start? Islam's itinerant work was the cause of everything. The encounter between the two took place about 25 years ago. Islam was shaving someone near Jannu Lal's house which is how they got to know each other. Since then, Islam and Jannu Lal have shared a great deal of their lives with each other. Jannu Lal, just a year or so younger than his friend, is actually Islam's *chacha*[5] because Jannu Lal and Islam's fathers look upon each other as brothers. Fictive kin relationships are not confined to these two individuals from both communities but as it is customary in villages, it usually extends to entire communities. I once encountered Jannu Lal in a large clearing between the two friends' villages where boys usually play cricket and *kabbadi*.[6] Jannu Lal was supervising the activity of a few Muslim young men in the process of sizing and warping silk yarn enough to weave four or five saris—an activity that is often seen in the Muslim *mohalla*s of Varanasi. I was curious about his role there and asked him what he was doing. He replied that he was helping them, and then turning to the boys he said, 'these are my children'. This sentence struck me as noteworthy because it had been spoken in such a natural manner. One time, I was sitting in front of Islam's house, and a

---

[5] Paternal uncle.
[6] An Indian national sport.

married young man from Jannu Lal's caste community and village, returning home through Islam's *mohalla*, stopped at our gathering and pointed at Shezadi, out of all the women present there, and told me that she was his *bhabhi*,[7] obviously implying a relation of brotherhood with Islam.

Jannu Lal has been a weaver all his life. He weaves the famous Banarsi brocade silk sari for a Muslim master weaver of Varanasi. Starting in the 1930s, Jannu Lal's community was initiated into weaving by the Muslim master weavers of the city and after a period of apprenticeship, handlooms were set up in their village. Jannu Lal belongs to the second generation of weavers in his village. In a history of consistent decline (and finally quasi-disappearance) of the craft in this village, Jannu Lal is one of the very few people left working for a Muslim master weaver. He learnt the profession from his father, again a weaver, at the age of 10. It took Jannu Lal one year to learn how to weave. In the second stage of his apprenticeship, he learned about the technical aspects of the loom from a Muslim teacher. At first, Jannu Lal worked for his father but then the Muslim master weaver asked Jannu Lal's father to send his son to work at his premises. Jannu Lal's family was too poor to turn down the request and so Jannu Lal was sent to work for the master weaver for a few years. Eventually, the latter set up a loom for him back in the village. Years later, Jannu Lal tried to start an independent business but the market was so unfavorable that he had to go back to weave for his former master. His relationship with his employer is still good, as he says it is based on a friendship that spans two generations. And when Jannu Lal used to go and deliver the saris to the master weaver, the latter would treat him with great trust. Lately, the business trends have worsened to the point that Jannu Lal had to resume his work at the master weaver's loom at his house near the city—commuting every day on his bicycle from the village—just like during his boyhood days.

Jannu Lal's social background is important to understand the relationship with his employer as well as the one with Islam. Jannu Lal belongs to a former 'Untouchable' Chamar caste. Those Chamar weavers who were hired by Varanasi Muslim master weavers pointed out that the latter did not practice untouchability and this, one can imagine, made working relations easier. Islam provides his services to a range of Hindu communities. Chamars however, unlike other communities, are served by Muslim barbers because

---

[7] Brother's wife.

Hindu ones refuse to provide them with their services. Ram, an elderly Chamar man from Jannu Lal's village, once told me about an encounter he had with a Hindu barber many years earlier. Although the barber worked near Ram's *mohalla*, he was very likely to be an outsider as he did not know Ram's caste identity. The barber started to shave Ram but while doing so, he realized (or was probably told by someone) that Ram was a Chamar. He immediately stopped shaving Ram who became upset. He had had only half his face shaven so he threatened to beat the barber unless he finished his job. Eventually Ram managed to persuade the barber to complete his shave.

In Jannu Lal's view, he has never had a Hindu friend like Islam and generally speaking, inter-caste friendships are not very common within the Chamar community with whom I carried out fieldwork. Jannu Lal once told me about his friendship with Ajay, from a middle-ranking agricultural caste in a nearby village. Several years ago, Jannu Lal's family used to cultivate some of Ajay's land as sharecroppers. Ajay considered Chamars as 'Untouchable' except for Jannu Lal. He and Ajay used to 'eat from the same *thali*'—a symbolic expression used to convey familiarity and the absence of caste bias—and they used to go to watch movies together. It is likely that Ajay was a true friend as eating together is often still a main barrier to social relations, at least in this geographical area. After Ajay's death years later, Jannu Lal gave up sharecropping.

Unlike his friendship with Ajay, Jannu Lal's friendship with Islam has no ideological implications—as there is no history of untouchability-based beliefs and practices between the two communities—and does not need to be explained along those lines. Rather, countless movies in the city's halls, marriages, Muslim and Hindu festivals have all been occasions where the two would turn up together. Similarly, Jannu Lal and Islam support each other at any time and sharing has been a hallmark of this relationship. The system of reciprocity they have created extends to their respective families too. When Islam became a grandfather Jannu Lal used to send him cow's milk and when Jannu Lal's last son was born, Islam used to reciprocate the favor by sending buffalo's milk to his friend. They also exchange food, like *roti* and *chatni* and whenever Jannu Lal cooks non-vegetarian food, he invites his friend. They used to spend time fishing together, however Jannu Lal does not eat fish. He catches fish for Islam because he likes it. On the other hand, for example, Jannu Lal gets free haircuts. Islam's help to Jannu Lal also concerns ritual events. Many years ago, on the occasion of the death of the latter's father, Islam performed *pinda-dan*[8] for the deceased. Again, a few years ago, I observed Islam supervising the wedding of Jannu Lal's daughter, ensuring—together with the women of the household—that those people directly involved in the ceremony followed the proper ritual procedure. Apart from these gestures of affection and ritual relations, there are also recriminations between these friends, for instance on Islam's side. Jannu Lal likes to eat *paan* in true Banarsi style, so Islam complains that the friend spoils him by making him eat *paan*. The *paan*-eating score however is always two-to-one in Jannu Lal's favor!

One might think Islam and Jannu Lal have become close friends by virtue of their shared marginality. This might well be true, especially given that the practice of untouchability, and the renewed modern forms which this practice takes, unfortunately still inform social relations as well as more general socio-economic considerations that apply to the communities of the two friends. However, if one were to spend time with them, one would very unlikely fail to miss the fact that despite their background of poverty, illiteracy and lack of resources, these two men have a certain status within their respective communities and outside them, and certainly would not bow to circumstances or people forcing them into 'marginal' positions. To Islam one thing is very clear: 'money is not everything', and he will not provide his services to people who do not give him adequate respect. On the other hand, Jannu Lal likes to remember how in his young days, he went to jail twice as a result of protesting for the rights of his *biradari* (caste community). Similarly, he is a respected member of the panchayat (caste council) in his village. These are certainly people whom development has not so far endowed with amenities like uninterrupted power, a telephone connection, or a fridge. However, there is an element of 'progress' in their speeches and whether this is a rhetorical exercise or not, no one apart from them can tell as no one else but them has seen changes in their respective communities as they have.

This friendship is better described by other features rather than mutual feelings of exclusion or an inferiority complex. I would think of their friendship as also encapsulating the common northern Indian expression of *len-den* (take and give), a system where reciprocity is inscribed in an intricate web of social relations which are ever reinforced by the exchange. A system of reciprocity which, in this case, does not leave much room for

---

[8] A post-cremation rite.

hierarchical principles along the lines of community. More importantly, their friendship is characterized by the emotional support that the two individuals gain in their everyday activities. Friendships, in Jannu Lal's view however, never last. They go on for a few years and then they come to an end. Both Islam and Jannu Lal claim, however, that they are not aware of a friendship like theirs in their large network of acquaintances. This is quite extraordinary given Islam's itinerant work and Jannu Lal's extreme sociability and therefore the large number of people they both know. But I am sure that social background was not the main *keyword* or criterion which they apply while trying to think of relationships that could resemble theirs, and they may as well have transcended community boundaries and searched only for mere 'friendships'.

My previous and limited experience of friendships between members of Muslim and Chamar communities is confined to the fine-grained description found in Rohinton Mistry's well-known novel *A Fine Balance.* Here, a Muslim tailor changes forever the fortunes of a Chamar family by teaching them his profession which will allow them to escape untouchability-ridden village life in colonial India. The Chamars' gratitude shows when, through a courageous act, they save the tailor and his family's lives from the communal violence that had spread in the wake of partition. As fiction often echoes lived experience, I believe that when both Islam and Jannu Lal claimed their friendship to be unique they were actually wrong, and many more of this kind exist, hidden to their eyes, or just waiting to be brought to light.

2

M's Book

1

M once told me that I had too many friends. 'Not just you', he said.
'The same goes for my brother and for Z, our neighbor. Too many
friends.' 'For myself', M said, then and again, 'friendship is a matter of
visvas.' Of trust. You have to believe in someone. 'And how many people will
you meet in your life that you can believe in?'

M had not wanted to get married. 'My wife is beautiful,' he said. She was
away from Lucknow at the time, in eastern Uttar Pradesh, where both her
and M's branch of the family were from. She was pregnant with their first
child: M's father, the poet, had brought her to her parents' home for the
summer as he had his other daughter-in-law. I didn't meet any of them at
the time, and the poet died not long afterwards. 'But how could I marry her?'
M would repeat. 'How could I have *visvas* with someone I barely knew?'

It was not that M was a modernist, at least not in terms of holding a brief
for love marriage. For him, the problem of a wife was the problem of the
friend, and simply adopting a different kind of marriage could not solve it.
M did have one friend, or so he let on. This was 'in Saudi'. M's one true friend
was his 'Honor', his employer for much of the decade he had worked in
Saudi Arabia and the Gulf as a driver. M was, at the time of the conversation
we were having, in his late twenties. Later he would speak of a second friend,

* Thanks to Mukulika Banerjee, Aditya Behl, Veena Das, Aaron Goodfellow, Shiv
Khan, Saleem Kidwai and Bhrigupati Singh for critical reflections on this text or on the
events constituting it.

and much later of a mysterious third, but these other, ultimately impossible, friendships were intimately bound up to what happened in Saudi.

2

The second friend: near the middle of the 1997 summer when I rented a *barsati*, a rooftop apartment, from the poet's family, M offered me this: 'Maybe I can have *visvas* with you.' The offer was risky, for though like M's Honor I was foreign and apart from the rest of his world, I was one of those with too many friends and by M's reckoning not enough belief in any of them. And friendship had become part of my work, a professional matter. I had come to Lucknow to work on a book that at the time I thought would be on friendship between men, sexual and otherwise. I was interviewing many men and women, usually in their homes with other friends or family present but when that was impolitic or inconvenient, at cafés or in parks. With a few men *aisa hai*, 'like this,' who some might call bisexual or gay and who on occasion did not feel as comfortable with a public meeting, we spoke in the rented *barsati*. M watched the men file in and out. 'You interview them?' he asked, repeating to me what I had earlier told him to explain the traffic. Yes. 'On friendship?' Yes. 'And on sex?' That too. 'And you get paid to do this, L?' Yes, well, sort of. 'And this is anthropology?' He laughed. Later, when M was repairing the light fixture above my door, he put in a new bulb, a red one. 'M, you know what a red light bulb means in my country?' 'I know, L,' he said, 'I lived in Saudi.' He paused. 'It means you're an anthropologist.'

But the offer of a serious friendship from M was not made lightly, and I tried to receive it in that spirit. M began to visit me, nights in the *barsati* before I went to bed, and we would talk. M was usually quiet in most company, save with his neighbor and relation Z's mother, to whom he was very close and went to often, when he was in Lucknow and not in Saudi, as a confidante: 'Only Z's mummy understands me.' I in contrast am often garrulous. But in the *barsati*, M would talk, on and on, and I would have to listen.

He talked of friendship, not surprisingly. I was trying to figure out how to write about it, and M had strong feelings. You don't need to talk to those other men, he told me. They are not telling you the truth. Listen to me. M described his Honor, his sole friend. M had worked in Dubai from the age of 14 and a few years later had gone to Saudi. The elder of two brothers, M was the only member of his immediate family who had gone. M's Honor became a father to him, and later, a friend. 'He took care of me. He respected me,' M said. 'I get paid twice what the other men, from Kerala, from Bombay, make. Because I work hard. I work from five in the morning to ten at night. And when I am working, it is all I think about. My Honor told me I am more valuable to him than 10 men.'

3

M never spoke of why he had been sent to Dubai as a 14-year-old by his father the poet and by his uncles, and thence to Saudi. But he had spent much of his life away from his immediate family, and even in the Lucknow house, he in many ways seemed to keep his distance. He had little interest in his father's work or in the painful past that the elegist's poems made present. In this he differed from their neighbor Z. If M was close to Z's mother, Z idealized M's father.

Z was a high-school teacher, and in the evenings he gave tutorials to his male students. He often talked of M's father with me. The poet was a renowned author of *marsia*, of the elegies that saturated both Shia devotion and the space of nostalgia and mourning that seemed so quintessentially *Lakhnavi*, of Lucknow. Z often spoke to me of what it *meant* for him to be Shia. It was a summer in which political brinksmanship between the three political parties struggling for power in the state capital—the Bharatiya Janata Party (BJP), the Bahujan Samaj Party (BSP), and the Samajwadi Party—had spilled over and ignited a series of deadly fights between Sunnis and Shias in the old city. Curfew was declared.

'If you are interested in these topics,' R (a society hostess) had suggested to me at a dinner party on still fashionable Mall Road (not under curfew), 'you should really study the Shias. I'm told much goes on in the Imambara on Moharram. They worship Husain you know, and the feeling of adoration spills over.' The conversation bothered me; I relayed it to Z. M wouldn't have been interested. 'They don't understand,' Z said, 'they' referring less to Mall Road soirée inferences of homosexuality or general élite Hindu and Western condescension than to the quite distinct Sunni accusations of idolatry he heard in them. 'We *don't* worship Husain, we *love* him.' And the cultivation of love, idealized and erotic, was part of what Z brought to his pedagogy, formally in the classroom, playfully at home in the tutorials.

In Z's case, such love was more than an everyday practice: it had become a *project*. Z was committed to institutionalizing a poetics of love that would not just remember but restore some lost possibility in the city: a kind of lost sociality. This project was experimentally articulated in several, unexpectedly overlapping ways. Z was a passionate, brilliant teacher. Z and a group of other men, both Hindu and Muslim, had helped found a fledgling gay group. The vision of the group's senior founder was forward-looking, and it drew upon new 'gay groups' that had recently been started in Bombay and Delhi and by Indian and other South Asian migrants, a decade earlier, in San Francisco, London and New York. Unlike these other groups the Lucknow group was more welcoming to and indeed was primarily constituted by married men in their forties and fifties, and its vision drew upon what one might term an ethics of patronage between older and younger men and was distinctively intergenerational. Z's own commitment to pedagogy dovetailed somewhat with that of these older men and the younger men they patronized, but he seemed always to have a wider sense of their place in history than did the others and, as he noted, a particularly Shia ethics of love that animated his commitments to both ongoing and new forms of care.

The possibility of such an ethics of loving commitment was for Z rooted in language, in particular that long *Lakhnavi* embrace of Urdu, and here his devotion to M's father had allowed Z to imagine Urdu's redemption. Z's tutoring, his everyday pedagogy, was in English. But together with the poet he planned to write a monumental history of the Urdu language; not merely he told me to recall forgotten writers but to save the language, to revive the embrace.

M appeared oblivious to the gay group that had formed around him, even though not only Z but M's younger brother H had become involved. Then again, Z, H, and I were united by the problem of *visvas*, of too many friends. M appeared even less interested in poetry, and in the writing of monumental treatises, than in friendship or marriage. When he spoke of language, which was seldom, he spoke not of Urdu, or Hindi or English, but of Arabic, in the daily use of which he unlike the rest of his family was fluent. He wanted to make more money in Saudi and to buy property, to become a contractor. H, married and with two children already, was something of a ne'er-do-well, and so the family looked to M for their future. But it was not so much with a sense of duty, of *farz*, that M would turn discussions of language and books into talk of work. Work, unlike books, was something in which you could have *visvas*.

The *barsati* was M's first project, as a future contractor, and I was its first occupant.

4

I came to Lucknow waving an invisible book. I had begun to think about questions of friendship, and love, and sexual difference in another Uttar Pradesh city, Banaras, where I had lived on and off from 1983 to 1993. But this thinking was entangled with the friendships, love affairs, and hardnesses of the heart that constituted it. Old friends began to look askance when I plumbed our shared histories as food for thought.

I had the idea that I could begin anew, find a place to work where I knew no one, and avoid the ethical confusions that my own project to be a professor of desire was producing. Lucknow made sense for many reasons, among which that it was like Banaras blessed with a flourishing sense of itself. Through friends of friends in the NGO (non-governmental organization) world, I contacted Z, and he mentioned that his neighbor was finishing building a *barsati*, and that he was looking for a tenant. Not wanting to repeat the awkwardness of Banaras, I announced my scholarly purpose to all and sundry. I was writing a book: get to know me at your peril. Any offers of care beyond some bare minimum—and in a city with such a cultivated sense of hospitality, these offers were frequent—were met by me at some point with a mention of the book. As M made his overtures, gracing me with the possibility of a trust he seemed seldom to extend, I reminded him of my textual intentions. M, I am interviewing you to be in the book. You cannot have *visvas* in me.

M didn't seem to be all that interested in the book, or my intentions. Despite them, each evening when he came by the *barsati* he saw that I was attentive and interested and clearly liked him.

H, his younger brother, had been the first of the brothers to visit the new tenant. H had little interest in friendship, in M's serious sense, but just in finding out whether I wanted to fool around. He had no problems with *visvas*. When their parents grew tired of M's continual deferrals of a wedding, they married off H, who was delighted. He and his wife immediately had a child, then a second. A few of H's friends met to go around some of the parks where they met other men for sex. They came to form the core of the younger men in the gay group Z had helped found. Unlike similar groups in Delhi or Mumbai, where the logic of group inclusion and exclusion as well as the erotics of difference seemed organized around class and the ability to speak English, exchanges and identities within the Lucknow group were structured around age. H liked the connection; it gave him easier access to older men who gave him presents and who demanded less of him than the poet did. Like his brother if for different reasons, H did not embrace the culture of Urdu and of *marsia*. He had a husband, an older man he met, a trader from the state of Bihar to the east who passed through Lucknow from time to time. H told me, ever alert to the possibility of new friends: 'he's like you, older, fair, fat, with a beard. I like that.' H got one of the senior members of the gay group to speak with me: 'The boy likes you. He's gay; so is the brother. Well, maybe not the brother: he's *different*. But the younger one is. He's married? So what. We're all married. This is India, *bhai*. So, are you interested?' I reminded the army man yet again that I was writing a book. 'To be honest,' he said, 'no one here cares about your bloody book. Are you interested or not?'

When M began to visit me, H ceased to appear. I had become his older brother's friend and off limits.

I never asked M if having too many friends was a way of speaking of a certain kind of fooling around, between men. His point seemed to lie elsewhere. Having too many friends was not about sex but about forms of involvement that M found untrustworthy. H had his gang and his older paramours, several of whom were uncles of some sort in the poet's large extended family. Z had his fellow activists, his students and his fellow teachers. I had all my informants, and the people I met at R's parties. What we shared, as M saw it, was a lack of *visvas*.

5

With each visit to the *barsati* at night, M would talk more about Saudi, his Honor, and his wife. He had been married on a visit back home, against his wishes. He returned soon after to Saudi and showed little inclination to return home. His family sent her, accompanied, to live with him. At times M spoke in his ascetic mode: 'I would not sleep with her. I did not know her, did not have *visvas*.' At other times, he spoke of their love playfully. 'My wife says that I am *Playboy*,' he said, one night after Z's birthday party that we had held in the *barsati* though M, always dour, was not invited. But there was liquor around, and M, who did not drink, decided unexpectedly he wanted to have some. Somewhat drunk after one peg, he described their marital love in far more passionate terms than his usual and frequent deferral. His wife had lived with the other women in the Honor's house, not in the workers' dormitory with him. They had to be creative to find places to meet. The *Playboy* reference was to the magazine, and the sense of the body, free sex, and spectacular address it conveyed. M drank some more, looked at me, and said 'do *you* think that I am *Playboy*?'

I looked at him, not sure how to respond. And M began to talk, once again, about his Honor. How His Honor had respected and loved him. How he had made M do things that he did not, at first, want to do, that he did not enjoy, but he did them anyway because his Honor did love him and they had this *visvas*. I was still. M sat next to me. 'I loved him,' he said, and we were no longer in the terrain either of marriage or of the various projects of love that were floating around the neighborhood among the men with too many friends.

'I loved him, I had *visvas*. He did these things, but he said he loved me. He gave me much more than the other workers, the ones from Kerala and Pakistan. And I worked for him, I never failed to work.' He paused. The house was silent, the party over, the poet and his two daughters-in-law all still away, and the few people downstairs asleep.

I did not know what to do. I put my arms around M. But he shook himself loose, stood up, and turned to me. '*You* say you are writing a book. My father writes books. Z is writing a book. Everyone is writing a book. Well, I am writing a book, more important than any of these.'

'L, you say your book is about friendship. What do you know about friendship? My book will tell the *truth* about friendship.'

Again, a long pause: M was thinking about something. He looked sick. 'I have a friend,' he finally said. Not his Honor, not me. And M told a story.

'My friend is also from here. He was with me, in Saudi. He had an Honor, who loved him. Or so his Honor said.'

'My friend's wife was in Saudi with him. She lived with the other women, and they had not been together. But then she became pregnant. He knew he could not have been the father; he knew who the father must have been.'

'This was his Honor, this was the man who had told my friend that he *loved* him. *This* was how he loved him. My friend was angry, and wanted his Honor to be punished. In Saudi there are strong laws. My friend wrote down all that he knew, all that his Honor had done to him, and to his wife. But then he was afraid: what if his Honor found the papers on which he had written all this, what if he had him killed? So he gave his book to me, to keep it safe. But *my* Honor found it. And he was enraged, and he threw the book into the fire. He told me never to publish this book.'

I started to say something, but M continued. 'This is the book that *must* be written. Not your book.'

'But I cannot write it. Who will read a book that *I* write? *You* must write it, L. In America, my Honor cannot stop it, and in America people will read it. *This* is the book that you must write. You must go back to America and write this book.' M pushed me down on the bed, and he threw up.

6

The week after I left Lucknow, M and his wife had a daughter. After a year at home with his new family, M returned to Saudi to work. I never wrote M's book, or my own, and for reasons I did not quite understand avoided going back to Lucknow. Several years passed. Power continued to shuffle between the BSP, BJP, and Samajwadi Party. The gay group Z was a part of was absorbed into a larger NGO, a leader nationally and internationally in AIDS prevention and research. To run the new organization, the director of the international NGO passed over the older group's senior-most founder (the man who had warned me that no one cared about my book) for a younger man who the director felt was more committed and capable. Humiliated, the older man broke away and started a new group.

Some time after, the city police were informed of possible infractions of the law by the new NGO. They swept in and arrested many of the AIDS outreach workers for alleged violations of obscenity and sodomy laws. Several persons in the AIDS world saw the handiwork of the displaced founder and his allies behind the arrests. The police seized foreign how-to safe-sex videos as evidence of criminal malfeasance. Though many human rights and AIDS activists around India and around the world became involved and argued that these charges were untenable even under the existing sodomy law, those arrested endured a harrowing, violent stay in prison. Some of the arrested included Z, a few of his former students, and M's brother H.

7

All this seemed far removed from M's concerns when I finally returned to Lucknow to see him. The *barsati* had been expanded into a separate apartment and a new *barsati* built on top of it. It was quite separate now from the downstairs house, where M's mother and H and his family still lived. The poet had died, and with him Z's plan for the revival of Urdu. M doted on his beautiful daughter, and spent much of his time watching American action pictures on a huge television set that he bought after his last Saudi trip and that dominated the family bedroom. We ate lunch while Americans took revenge on the Japanese in *Pearl Harbor*, and then M's little girl sang 'Twinkle Twinkle Little Star' for us. M told me he had sent her to one of the best convent schools in the city so that she would have a chance in life. 'I will not have any more children,' he said. 'If you have a child, you must be able to give him a future. So we will have one child only.' I knew some of the teachers at this school; recently, one had told me she overheard two girls talking in the schoolyard. 'My mother said not to play with her,' one had said to the other. 'She's a *Muslim*.' It was three months after the massacres in Gujarat. The teacher, also Muslim, had not said anything.

V, to me *bhabhiji*, M's wife, brought in a beautiful cake from a bakery that had my name written on it. When she left, I asked M how his return to Saudi was. He smiled and told me how much more he made there than other drivers, and how hard he worked for his Honor. But visas, he said, were increasingly hard to obtain, especially from Lucknow. Perhaps I might know of jobs for drivers in America? While I detailed my failed efforts to get other friends through the increasingly prejudicial wall of US immigration, we watched Ben Affleck bomb the Japanese.

8

I read some of this essay to friends, fellow academics, and one of them was struck by M's use of *visvas*, or my rendering of it: it struck, she felt, a false note.

What might have been at stake, in that receding summer, in the matter of trust, of friendship as a relation of belief? Certainly, M's claims for the difficulty of any authentic relation of care, whether those of friendship or marriage, spoke to my own concerns about the relation of affection and research. They seemed, as I came even slightly to know him, to come out of the crucible of one young man's experience as a socially marginal migrant and from conditions of value and belonging thereof that did not easily translate back in Lucknow. They emerged during the summer of a pregnancy that invoked some anxiety, perhaps in ways that go beyond the fears attributed to a friend. They took the form, one evening, of a lost book, and of a demand that I find a way to rewrite it.

The year after V and M gave me the beautiful cake, I returned to see them again. The *barsati* had been further enlarged and M and I sat in a small courtyard surrounded by family and new tenants. We did not talk about *visvas*. We did talk of Saudi, but M only spoke of the increasing bureaucracy he had to negotiate to obtain his work visas. He and I speculated as to the regional and global forces that determined visa availability. He was not sure if he would be able to take up his job as a driver. Some months later, I received an email from one of M's tenants, letting me know that M had finally made it back and had landed, that very day, in Saudi.

Dare I make broader claims for *visvas*, for the space and time of its failure? Am I suggesting an allegory, for communalism and the commitment to a future for Muslims in Lucknow? Or am I speaking to something else, something at stake in the care and violence of portraiture under liberalism and my heeding, here, its siren song? I will have to figure it out: I am writing a book, perhaps the wrong one.

3

The *Alim* and the Anthropologist
Rethinking with the Help of an Unlikely Informant

3

The *Alim* and the Anthropologist
Rethinking with the Help of an Unlikely Informant

BRIAN J. DIDIER

What puzzles me is not why bad things are done by bad people, but rather why bad things are done by people who otherwise appear to be good...by pious people dedicated to a moral vision of the world.[1]

Part I: The Anthropologist

I must admit that I was intimidated. For the first time in my year-long research within the Muslim community of Androth Island I was a bit unnerved at the thought of conducting an interview. I had been on Androth—the largest of the tiny coral atolls in the Arabian sea that make up India's Union Territory of Lakshadweep—for about nine months, and much of that time was spent trying to get information on a mysterious conflict that was adversely affecting island social and religious life. Mosque closures, armed police officers, whispered accusations and fractured families suggested

[1] Mark Juergensmeyer, 2000, *Terror in the Mind of God: The Global Rise of Religious Violence*, Berkeley: University of California Press, p. 7.

that something strange was happening and I proceeded cautiously in investigating an island phenomenon that no one wanted to talk about.

Over the course of my year on this island I discovered that it was an ongoing 30-year-old religious dispute that was producing deep social fissures and cracks in the religious congregation. The conflict climaxed in 1986, 10 years before my arrival on the island and nearly 20 years after the dispute began. During that pivotal year a harmless quarrel over ritual and doctrinal matters between two factions of the Sunni population erupted into a rather nasty confrontation. The catalyst, it seems, was a *fatwa* issued by the island religious clerics or *ulema*. In this collectively authored *fatwa*, the *ulema* condemned a separate group of islanders—a Sufi brotherhood known as the Shamsiyya—for their un-Islamic behavior. In essence, the Androth *ulema* accused the Shamsiyya of being heretics or *kafirs*. While the *fatwa* itself mentions nothing about any punishment or persecution, supporters of the clerics were determined that the condemnation in words should be coupled with forceful social sanctions. Shortly after the *fatwa* was issued, the Shamsiyya followers were prevented from entering the island's Juma Masjid and other neighborhood mosques. They responded by challenging the expulsion. According to witnesses, a brief outbreak of violence erupted as the two groups tussled outside the Friday mosque. What I witnessed during my stay on the island was the social fallout of that conflict. The mosques were closed to prevent any more confrontations and the police were there to ensure that peace was maintained. The whispered accusations of heresy were still directed at members of the condemned Sufi brotherhood. Split families and divorced couples represented the social fallout of the religious fracture.

After months of research and interviews one set of questions remained unanswered: Why would the island *ulema* feel compelled to condemn fellow islanders and condone such forms of persecution? Of course, the responsibility for the conflict must be spread widely. Members of the Shamsiyya were certainly not innocent of being antagonistic. Much of the blame for what happened must also lie with members of the general public, many of whom either supported the *ulema* in the accusation or actively participated in the mosque expulsions and the later alienation of the Shamsiyya. No amount of apportioning blame, however, can hide the fact that it was the island *ulema* who were instrumental in creating the conflict and pushing it towards incivility.

The problem, however, was that the answers to these questions required that I confront the *ulema* on their behavior. And to be quite frank, I was afraid to do so. I was intimidated. What did I fear? Mostly, I was afraid that they would find my questions offensive or too sensitive and that they would become quite agitated. I assumed that the same kind of aggressive response exhibited in the conflict would be directed towards me, the overly inquisitive and brazen anthropologist. I imagined them thinking or perhaps even saying: 'What right did you—a foreigner, an American, a young adult and a non-Muslim—have to question our decisions on religious matters?' Anger and animosity, particularly coming from men of such local prominence, could ruin my remaining research and bring a quick end to my island welcome. So I procrastinated.

Was I justified in fearing their wrath? No. But I will try to explain the source of my anxieties anyway. Coming of age in America in the late 1970s and early 1980s, my only experience of Islam or its clerics was through the searing television images of ayatollahs urging death to America and any fiction writers who dared to portray Islam in a negative light. My time on Androth in 1998–99 was not only my first fieldwork experience, but it was also the first time I had had any extended contact with Muslims. Any knowledge regarding Islam that I brought to the island was either out of some book read in graduate school or what remained of that media-induced specter that haunted my adolescence. Unfortunately, the beards, robes and severe expressions worn by so many of the island *ulema* only confirmed a stereotype I had unwittingly carried with me. Feeding into my insecurities and biases was the fact that the *ulema* appeared to be so unfriendly. The clerics I passed in the street or encountered in a tea stall never greeted me with a friendly nod or smile as the other islanders did. When I asked a friend about such behavior, which I took to be discourteous, his reply was simple: 'Don't take it personally, they don't smile at anyone.'

And so it was that my long-standing and deep-seated biases, my liberal cynicism regarding public religion or passionate conviction, my slight knowledge of *ulema*'s previous conflict behavior, and my limited and uncomfortable island encounters combined to produce a stereotype. My impression of Islamic clerics—be they Indian-island *ulema* or Iranian ayatollahs—was that they were generally dour, narrow-minded (or at least narrowly trained) intolerant and quick to anger. My impression was that they were judgmental and heavy-handed in their response to dissent, whether expressed by a defiant Sufi or some insolent anthropologist. I soon discovered, however, how silly, exaggerated and unjust such stereotypes could be.

Part II: The *Alim*

Of course, I now regret that such biases delayed my meeting with the *ulema* and thus shortened the time I could spend with them. As it is, I'll have to wait for a return visit before pursuing those initial conversations. It was my fieldwork assistant and close friend—a man everyone called PPC—who finally convinced me that anxieties must be set aside and the ultimate interviews be conducted. PPC made the arrangements and our destination was the home of one of the islands' most prominent and respected *ulema*. This man—let us call him Koya—was also one of the authors of the *fatwa* of condemnation and thus integral to the story of the Androth conflict. While PPC and I would meet with other island *ulema* over the summer of 1998, it was the conversations with Koya that transformed how I think about religious conflict and the religious authorities so often at the center of them.

The delay was most regrettable because when I finally met with this most influential *alim*, I found him to be extraordinarily friendly and a most engaging conversationalist. On three occasions we talked into the early hours of the morning about Islam, America and my impressions of island life. We would arrive at his modest house late at night. In addition to being a cleric, Koya was also a shopkeeper. While running the store kept him at work until quite late, he never seemed bothered to receive us upon returning home. I should point out that the home we visited was not actually Koya's; it was his wife's. This is one of the curious things about the island's matrilineal kinship and residential system. Upon marriage, the women of the island usually reside in the lineage home. Married men stay in their lineage home during the day (with their brothers, sisters and their sister's children) and visit their wives and children at night. Every evening there is a kind of great migration as brothers leave the lineage home (to visit their wives) and husbands arrive. In the morning, it is the reverse: husbands depart and brothers return. Koya, like most other married men on the island, was a guest in his wife's home.

In addition to being a prominent cleric and a shopkeeper, Koya was also a devoted husband and father. This side of him came out numerous times in our conversations. Many of his questions focussed on my own family. I recall him asking me with genuine concern how it is that I could live so far from family and friends and for such a long time. My year of solo fieldwork spent on the islands struck him as a deeply lonely enterprise. The time I spent away from my family—attending college, working in a different city or conducting fieldwork—troubled him.

There was no such solitude in this house. Our conversations were regularly interrupted by Koya's adoring and jovial wife, who ensured that tea was always flowing and that she had a say in our conversations. Standing in a doorway with a shawl draped over her head, she would tease PPC while Koya sat grinning. I found such informal banter between the four of us particularly refreshing. When arriving at the homes of so many other island friends, the women would scamper behind a door or curtain to maintain *purdah*. At many homes, my only interaction with adult sisters or wives was to glimpse a shadowed face peeking through a window or to watch a covered arm with snacks in hand extending out from behind a curtain. Yet here in the home of this learned and pious cleric, the woman of the house felt free to wander in and out and to participate in our conversation. Was Koya particularly lenient when it came to *purdah*? Was his wife simply being comfortable in what was her own home? Or was she of such age and standing that seclusion no longer mattered? I didn't ask. I just enjoyed the rare informality of it all.

Our conversations also covered many aspects of local Islam. Koya was, after all, an *alim*—one of Islam's traditional guardians and interpreters of Islamic scripture and law, and I valued his guidance and instruction in a religion that was still relatively new to me. Before asking him about the sensitive issue of the island conflict, I thought it best to begin with other questions about island religious rituals and practices. Two practices in particular fascinated me and had long set island religion apart from that of many other Muslim communities. The first of the cultural practices that I found quite curious was their system of matrilineal descent known as *marummakathayam*. Once prominent among the Hindu Nayar caste of neighboring Kerala, this unique social system is now curiously preserved by many of the Muslim communities in Lakshadweep. Very few societies in the world today practice matriliny. Muslim matriliny is even rarer. Arab culture is strictly patrilineal and the Prophet Mohammed traced his descent through his father. Inheritance rules prescribed in the Quran are patrilineal as well. In a matrilineal system such as the islanders', however, one traces descent through the mother and takes her family name. Similarly, one inherits the family property of the mother's lineage, not the father's. Many Muslims on the Malabar Coast and elsewhere have criticised such practices, arguing that at best they are unconventional, at worst unwarranted and abhorrent departures from Islamic law. Koya was certainly familiar with such arguments and even admitted that in a strict sense matriliny did not adhere to *shariah* law and thus was an innovation. He did not admit, however, that the islanders were poor or less adequate Muslims on account of it. According to him, the islanders' matriliny was an acceptable innovation, harmless and thus not un-Islamic. Moreover, it was a social fact and custom. What could they do, get rid of it? In fact, he argued, dispensing with the system in order to adhere more strictly to the patriliny of Islamic law would be the greater injustice to Islam. His logic, which I found quite compelling, was that making such fundamental change to island kinship system would cause social and economic chaos. Lineages would be disrupted and property rights contested. According to him, 'the Prophet would surely disapprove of such a social disturbance'.

The second practice that I discussed with Koya were the ecstatic rituals conducted by island mystics or Sufis. In these rituals the participants drum, chant, dance and pierce themselves with knives and skewers in order to achieve altered states of consciousness or divine ecstasy. Again, many critics and Islamic reformists have argued that such Sufi practices are dangerous innovations and that the practitioners are pseudo-Muslims or *kafir*s. According to this logic, knowledge or experience of the divine is to be channeled through Islamic law and standard forms of worship. There is no precedent for these ecstatic rituals in the Quran or in *shariah* law and thus they are un-Islamic. Koya's argument, however, was that such rituals were acceptable and even commendable as long as they were conducted under the authority of a recognized Sufi sheikh and conducted in a pious frame of mind.

A number of principles, it seems to me, were guiding Koya's stance on these issues. The first was a profound respect for tradition. Such practices as those discussed were conventional, bequeathed to the islanders by pious forefathers (and foremothers) and thus should not be belittled or dismissed lightly. Second, it seems that Koya placed serious stock in social harmony as an Islamic virtue. At least in the cases of matriliny and ecstatic Sufi rituals, narrow or legalistic interpretations of Islamic law should not necessarily trump convention or the prevention of disruptive social conflict. Apparently, slight deviations from the prescriptions of Islamic law or harmless innovations were not things to get too excited about. Thus, the Islam advocated by Koya seemed to be one that could accommodate minor deviations or innovations.

Part III: The Puzzle

After these first few interviews, the picture of the island *ulema* and that of Koya in particular had become more positive, more realistic yet also more cloudy. What happens when the minor deviations appear to become major, when the harmless innovations become dangerous? What happens if some in the community disagree with the interpretations of the *ulema*? How do the *ulema* deal with dissent, nonconformity or behavior they take to be seriously un-Islamic or dangerous to the integrity of the Islamic community? I was certainly happy to discover that the stereotypes regarding narrow-minded and dogmatic *ulema* had proven too simplistic. However, I still had to reconcile the fact that, on the one hand, Koya and his colleagues could be so tolerant and flexible when it came to matriliny or ecstatic Sufi practices, yet on the other hand be so narrow-minded and provocative when it came to the issue of confronting the Shamsiyya. Was Koya simply a contradiction, a man capable of some rather glaring inconsistencies when it came to defending religious orthodoxy? Was he a hypocrite, saying one thing to the anthropologist and doing something else? Or does the riddle have a more charitable answer?

When I finally mustered the confidence to broach the subject of the island conflict, Koya's replies continued to astound me. First, he responded with no blistering condemnation or fervent attack on the Shamsiyya designed to sway the opinion of the inquisitive anthropologists. Rather, his response was calm and measured. He patiently explained to me how his opposition and that of his clerical colleagues arose in the 1960s in reply to some ritual innovations introduced by the Shamsiyya founder and first sheikh. How did they respond? According to Koya: 'We cannot say that a man is out of Islam without a deep and constant study. We tried in a way to advise them [the Shamsiyya] in the beginning. We never tried to oppose. When these people started propagating among the public, trying to attract others, even then we didn't oppose. Then they brought someone from the mainland [an *alim* from Kerala] to propagate and discuss these matters. They brought scholars from the mainland and began speaking in public against us. Then we were compelled to oppose.'

Much has been said here. I should note that Koya's response supports what I had begun to discover about the evolution of the conflict. The *fatwa*, for example, was hardly a reactionary impulse. In fact, it was long in coming. Moreover, there were responses to the Shamsiyya's perceived infidelities that involved much more (or rather much less) than harsh condemnation or coercive violence. What Koya said—'that we tried to advise them in the beginning'—pushed me to explore further the early days of the conflict. I learned that soon after the Shamsiyya emerged as an active brotherhood, numerous island clerics were warning them about questionable ritual practices. It appears that such fraternal admonishment is a strategy often used to confront questionable practices. It's usually done in private and allows the accused to reply or defend themselves. I also learned that in 1980 the island *ulema* agreed to participate in a public debate over the issue of ritual innovation and infidelity with the mainland clerics who supported Shamsiyya. Such advisement, 'deep and constant study', and public debate are hardly the hallmarks of rash spontaneity. The picture that was emerging was not one of a hasty or furious reaction to dissent from within the community, but a calculated, flexible and gradual response to unorthodox behavior and dissidence and a moderate position on the discipline required to deal with it.

What is clear, however, is that the island *ulema* had limits. Perfectly willing to debate and persuade, they were also willing to condemn and punish. What was the trigger? If Koya is to be believed, the dynamic that set their resolve and compelled them toward coercion was not simply that the Shamsiyya had engaged in questionable ritual practice, but that they had challenged the authority of the established island *ulema*. That the Shamsiyya did this by using other *ulema* from the mainland was apparently a challenge the *ulema* could not ignore. Even tolerant men can lose their patience.

What about the *fatwa* of condemnation, the mosque expulsion and the violence that followed? Why couldn't the island *ulema* find some other way to deal with the affront? To these questions I received no direct answers. Koya neither laid the blame on some over-zealous supporters nor argued that the Shamsiyya deserved what they got. He told me that there was no doubt in his mind that the Shamsiyya were *kafir*s and un-Islamic. Their ritual innovations combined with their direct challenge to the island *ulema*'s authority proved, at least in the minds of the island clerics, that the Shamsiyya were a corrosive and un-Islamic force. When I pushed him on the *fatwa* and subsequent violence, he said nothing and grimaced while shaking his head in what I took to be a gesture of remorse. In my notebook I wrote that I sensed a degree of regret, not for the *fatwa* or the condemnation, but for the way the whole conflict had turned out. Surely, I thought to myself, the social fractures and religious fissures, the mosque closures and divorced couples were not exactly what the *ulema* intended. The ultimate irony here is that a measured response designed to preserve island orthodoxy and the integrity of the Islamic community ended up fracturing what it was meant to protect. And in that shake of the head, I sense that this *alim* in particular was living uncomfortably with the consequences.

4

Javeedbhai

THOMAS BLOM HANSEN

When I began my work in this dense, predominantly Muslim neighborhood in 1996, the renaming of the city was new. We were definitely still in 'Bambai', not in Mumbai. The memories of those awful months in 1992–93 were still fresh: the anger, humiliation and disbelief when the Babri Masjid was razed to the ground on 6 December 1992; the brutality of the Bombay police in suppressing the protests in the days after; the horrible 10 days in the beginning of January 1993 when the Shiv Sena and their supporters, burned, raped, looted and killed in Muslim neighborhoods all over the city, often protected by the police force. All this was capped by the multiple bomb blasts in March 1993 and the waves of arrests, beating and imprisonment of anyone suspected of even the most remote connection with the Muslim gangsters who allegedly planned and carried out the attacks.

What was I doing there, in that neighborhood? I had some local friends, and I had been around in the neighborhood for some weeks two years earlier when I helped a TV crew shoot a documentary about the rise of the Shiv Sena, the riots and their aftermath. Emotions were even more raw at that time in 1994. The attendance at Friday *namaz* in the local *masjid* had been massive, thousands of men standing silently in straight rows, shoulder-to-shoulder, traffic at a standstill for hours. A heroic, angry display of defiance and community, in the face of what seemed like relentless attacks by the state and powerful political forces.

There was apprehension regarding my intentions. Was I really a friend of Muslims? Could one really trust this *firangi* who stayed in the neighborhood, walked around and talked to so many people about religion, the riots, their work in the Gulf and so on. Was I actually some kind of journalist, like some of my local friends? Or did I have links with the government which at the time had been taken over by the Shiv Sena? Why was I so interested in Muslims, after all? After some time various people began to ask me if I had met Javeedbhai. They told me that he was an important man but someone who was not easy to meet, not just like that.

I became intrigued by this man and his reputation. Some of my friends advised me not to mix with him. He was a murderer, I was told, someone with a criminal record. I was not convinced that this really had any bearing on reality. To file an affidavit and claim that someone had committed a crime was after all one of the most well-tested ways to tarnish the reputation of an adversary, a political opponent or a business rival. An affidavit, some rumors and a bit of persuasion, pecuniary or not, is after all often enough just to make the police open a chargesheet against a person, who then enters the category of 'chargesheeter', an alleged criminal. However, with Javeedbhai it was different. He was a former convict and had been to prison for years. Others told me that he was just a proud man who always defended his neighborhood and that was the reason why the police resented him. They did not like strong and proud Muslim men, so he was framed and sent to prison.

This was the version of Javeedbhai's story I heard one day when I was sitting in a small workshop in an area full of little factories, power-loom sheds and small eateries in the neighborhood. One of the men I was chatting with was called Junaid. He claimed he was a friend of Javeedbhai. Junaid was a heavily built balding man in his fifties. His face had deep furrows, his eyebrows were bushy and almost met above his nose. This gave him a somewhat sinister look which he seemed quite pleased with. He claimed that he had acted in several Hindi movies, always as a gangster or evil man, he said, using the English word 'villain' again and again, as a matter of pride. He came from the same town in Uttar Pradesh (UP) as Javeedbhai and they had arrived at the same time in Bombay, as boys. They went back a long time and that was why Javeedbhai had always helped him. I asked him in what way he had helped. Junaid became a bit evasive but mentioned that he had had financial difficulties, and that he had been in trouble with the law when he was younger. Javeedbhai had always supported him and Junaid would always be loyal to him, no matter what people said about him.

Junaid promised to introduce me to Javeedbhai but whenever we met in the following weeks, there was always a problem, something had come up.

It turned out that a small incident that had taken place a few weeks after my arrival made a difference. I had stayed at a small guest-house for some time. The bigger rooms were all occupied by a group of Arab men from Kuwait and the Emirates. Officially they were in Bombay to recruit labor for their homes and businesses, but liquor and the nearby red light district seemed to preoccupy them more than anything else. Judging from their rude behavior, the men did not hold the local Muslims in high esteem. One evening, one of the men got into an argument with an elderly and frail looking taxi driver and started to assault him with his walking stick. A rage that had accumulated as I had watched the men's racist behavior over several weeks made me angrier and more stubborn than I had imagined. I intervened, got between him and the terrified taxi driver, and asked the owner of the guest-house to call the police. The Arab man was probably as surprised as I was, but quickly disappeared, shouting and swearing at me. I did not think much of it at the time but the incident obviously created a certain amount of goodwill and much of the apprehension about me began to vanish.

One evening, weeks after the incident, I was at a public meeting called by the local branch of the radical Islamic SIMI (Student's Islamic Movement of India) in the vicinity. Most of the young men present were college students, very serious and very keen on engaging me in debate. A group of smartly dressed young men were hanging around the door and as I was leaving one of them came up to me and asked me in English if I was the guy who had 'beaten up the Arab guy?' I told them that it was all a bit exaggerated but yes, there had been a minor scuffle. They smiled approvingly and told me that they thought *gussa* (anger) was a good quality in a man, a sign of proper manliness (*mardangi*).

One of the boys, Hanif, turned out to be Javeedbhai's son. Hanif went to the local Muslim college and had made friends with some of the SIMI activists. He admired them for their determination and strong convictions and he supported them. 'We have to stand up to the Shiv Sena and the BJP. They want to force all of us out of India, they don't allow us to be Muslims, but SIMI is showing young people that if we live according to the Quran, they can never beat us.' He admitted that he was not a good Muslim all the time but that he wanted to be a businessman like his father. He did not have the patience and discipline to study the *hadith*, learn Arabic and so on, like the SIMI activists. 'I am more like my father, someone who helps people and who has courage (*sahas*), who stands up for himself.' Knowing fully well that I knew the rumors about his father, he continued: 'People will tell you that my father is a gangster, a *dada*, and that he does not deserve respect…but when they are in trouble they come to him for help….'

Hanif promised to set up a meeting with his father, and the day after, he left a message that I should meet Javeedbhai in his office not far from where I stayed. Hanif was waiting outside and invited me inside Javeedbhai's modest office below his apartment in an old building in the crowded and busy lanes. Javeed was a handsome, athletic and energetic man in his fifties with a pleasant smile and a firm handshake. The room had a desk with two telephones, a small settee, an aerial photograph of the Kaba with masses of pilgrims, and a big painting of a tiger above the settee. Hanif's elder brother and three associates of Javeedbhai were present. After our tea and the usual pleasantries I asked, half-jokingkly if his tiger was stronger than the Sena tiger? The men all burst into laughter and Javeedbhai said 'Yes, of course, it is a Khan, like all of us…each of us are as good as five sainiks.' He spoke quickly, in clipped and succinct sentences and rarely elaborated or spoke at length. Hanif added that 'if only the police would leave us alone, let the Sena come here, man to man, and we shall see who are the real men.'

This seemed to be the pattern between father and this, his eldest son. Javeed would say something, a command, a small joke, and Hanif who always was extremely attentive to his father's whims and moods, would pick it up and elaborate, effortlessly switching between Hindi and English as do so many young people in Mumbai. While Javeed was tight-lipped—even as he smiled—controlled and austere in his appearance (always dressed in *kurta-pyjama*), his son had an open and friendly face and dressed smartly in expensive shirts and trousers. Javeed's face sometimes showed a thin smile when his son spoke eloquently and he was clearly proud of his son's manners and polish. The tiger theme returned in the coming months and became a bit of a joke. Javeedbhai told me that he considered using it if he decided to run for the post as municipal corporator in the local ward in the elections in the following year.

It turned out that Javeedbhai was very well informed about my whereabouts in the neighborhood. Who I stayed with, where I normally had my meals, which mosques I had been to, and which of his friends (and foes) I had met. We quickly developed a good rapport, laughed a lot and exchanged jokes. He wanted to know about my country, my previous work, about how Bal Thackeray was, the Sena leaders I had met, and so on. He was also interested in what local people had said about him and I recounted some of the more flattering stories about him. I jokingly called him 'Special Branch' when I realized how precisely he knew my whereabouts and I told him that he should apply for the job of Chief of the Special Branch in the Bombay Police. This nickname was also picked up by some of his associates who, at least in my company, and probably to flatter me, referred to this joke again and again.

As I got to know Javeedbhai better, I understood the full extent of his authority and how much respect he commanded in the locality. It was respect, first and foremost. Although I saw many signs of affection, Javeed commanded and expected unconditional loyalty from his men. His sons, especially Hanif, were often with him in his car or when overseeing his business. It was clear that Javeed was proud of both of them and that not least the younger one, 17-year-old Shahid, was allowed to joke and interrupt conversations in ways that none of Javeed's men would ever dare to do.

Javeed's own biography was typical of many in the locality, and yet distinctly different. He came to Bombay from a village in Uttar Pradesh as a young boy. His father had been working in a mill for years and had returned once a year to visit his family. As the children were growing, his father decided to bring his three sons to Bombay while his wife and two daughters stayed back for another few years until he found a suitable house for the entire family. Javeed lived with his father, brothers and uncles for some years. His brothers soon got jobs in the mills but his father decided that Javeed should continue his studies. He did not object but was envious of his brothers who earned money and could buy new clothes and go to the talkies. Instead Javeed took up wrestling at the local YMCA gymkhana. He turned out to have a real talent for wrestling and he soon became the favorite of the old Ustad who trained the boys and young men. Javeed was not a big man, but his strength, agility and especially his will to win made him a feared and respected *pehlwan*. At the age of 18 he had won several local championships and the Ustad hoped that he would climb further and achieve a national status as he himself had done in his day.

Javeed has been admitted to the local Muslim college and was doing well when misfortune struck the family. His father met with an accident at the mill and became crippled and confined to his bed for many years. The younger uncle was sent back to manage the family property in the village and to settle some disputes over inheritance. It fell upon Javeed's elder brother to take charge of the family's affairs. He invested the compensation paid to the father from the mill in a small metal workshop in the neighborhood. A barely literate man of limited capacity, he soon began to rely on Javeed's advice in virtually every matter. Javeed had left college and had taken various jobs to support his father and the family. Javeed recalled these years as bewildering and difficult and he was greatly pained by his father's protracted illness and early death. At the age of 25 Javeed was effectively managing the expanding metal workshop. His education and strong will made him the natural head of the family, something that created apprehensions and tension between him and his uncles and brothers. Although his wrestling career was at a standstill, he was still feared and respected in the street and greatly admired by many young men in the neighborhood.

'My uncles found a nice girl from our village in UP. They hoped that this would calm me down' he told me with a smile. But the inevitable happened. When you make money and become visible, someone will become jealous of you. For Javeed these two things—*dikhna* (visibility) and *jalna* (envy)—were linked like light and darkness. A local *dada* (strongman, sometimes the term *bhai* is also used, as a synonym for gangster/bad guy) had threatened Javeed's brother and wanted money from his thriving business. Javeed interpreted this demand as a challenge to him and his family. It became a tug of war, a battle of wills. Javeed refused to pay while his brothers thought it was unwise to stir trouble. It was well known that the local dada was a friend of the police, and that the police received handsome *hafta* (illicit payment in return for favor/ protection) from him to let him carry on with his extortion racket. This made him a dangerous man. But for Javeed it was now about honor (*izzat*), both his family's and his own honor and self-respect as a man.

One afternoon, the *dada* and two men came to the shop to demand money. Javeed exploded in rage, chased them out and confronted the *dada* with a knife in the street. A few seconds later the *dada* was lying on the pavement, bleeding profusely and dead shortly after. Javeed was arrested, tried and sentenced to life imprisonment. Prison life was harsh (*sakht*) but Javeed survived and became a different man, less proud but without fear (*dar nahi hai*). I heard several versions of this story. Some portrayed Javeed as local hero and protector of the neighborhood while others painted him as a thug aspiring to be the new *dada*. All versions agreed on one thing, however. Javeed had courage, lots of it, to the point of foolhardiness. He had confronted the *dada* and his men alone, face to face, and could have been killed himself had it not been for his superior fighting skills and his aggressiveness. The two accomplices had fled the scene, terrified by Javeed's ferocity. Some of the interlocutors of this story told me that such a fight could never happen today because all the *bhai* carry guns and don't have this kind of courage anymore, and by implication, deserve no respect either. Javeed's story was another instance of the deplorable condition of the Muslim community, its constant sliding into decay and weakness—the larger story that seems so pervasive in many parts of the subcontinent.[1]

He appeared completely reconciled with the killing and the punishment, however. 'What happened had to happen ... either you stand up as a man worthy of respect (*adarniya admi*) or you live like a servant. I did what I did and I have also paid for it.'

Javeed got out of prison after less than eight years but it was a bit unclear why it happened. All he told me was that he had shown good behavior and that someone had taken pity on him and his family. It seemed quite clear that he was indebted to someone, an influential man, who had been able to pull strings and get him released well ahead of time. The network of respect and dependency he was entangled in beyond the locality was one of the many dimensions of his life I never got to know about. I was only shown, and told about, his local reputation, the 'social work' he carried out (he always used the English term), and of course his family obligations and his obligations to his *biradari* in Bombay and in UP. Yet, these wider networks, some established while in prison, others after, were hugely important to his business and to his more recent attempts at a career in politics.

When Javeed returned from prison he was a changed man, more judicious and cautious but also more determined to recreate his life, his reputation and the honor of his family. In that he was helped by the way his reputation had developed and grown in his absence. He left the streets as a proud and arrogant young man but returned as a fully evolved *dada*, a strongman with extensive networks, as a man who had endured the ordeal of imprisonment. His brother's business had deteriorated in Javeed's absence and his brother survived mainly on the money which his son sent from Kuwait. Javeed set up a new business and gradually built a life for himself and his family. The business grew and soon Javeed evolved as a local man of eminence. People began to ask him for help with troublesome landlords and employers and he enjoyed his new status as a 'social worker', someone whose word, or presence, could solve problems. The more respectable and educated families in his neighborhood despised him intensely, however. They would never

---

[1] Sudhir Kakar describes the melancholic feeling of decay and loss of *hukumat* (the will/ability to rule) among Muslims in Hyderabad (Kakar 1996).

dream of approaching him or asking for his help. Rumor had it that he was not a proper Khan, although his surname was Khan. 'He is just a *julaha*' I was told several times by people referring to the traditional, and derogatory, name for the north Indian Ansari weaving community that made up a majority of the population in the locality and who had worked in the textile mills. 'His father changed his name when he came to Bombay', I was told by high-status Khans who only grudgingly accepted the gradual elevation of the *Julaha*/Ansaris to the status of proper Muslims. Some Khans felt that the name taken by this community—Ansari (Arabic for the helpers of the Prophet)—in itself was a provocation.

Javeed was acutely aware of the precariousness of his own reputation and he consistently downplayed the fact that his efficacy as a 'social worker' was built on a reputation for violence. It was widely assumed that because he had been to prison, and had been released early, he had multiple connections with the underworld. As elsewhere in the world, the assumption in central Bombay was that 'you go to prison as a local boy and return as a *bhai* (gangster)', as a friend put it to me.

Javeed tried to build up a more respectable image of himself. He claimed that the experience in prison had taught him humility and to respect Allah. He went to the local mosque now and then, and was adamant that his sons should grow up knowing about the faith (*din*). Both his sons and his daughters had attended a local English-medium convent school, and both the boys had been sent to the *madrasah* from an early age. None of them had become particularly observant Muslims but Hanif was very sympathetic to a broadly Islamist ideology, mostly because of its message of strength and assertion of identity.

Javeed donated money to several local *madrasahs* as well as to his old gymkhana although he was unhappy with the new caretaker. 'He allows all these rich boys from Bandra to use our facilities.... They come in their Marutis to do bodybuilding and all that...our young boys just hang around doing nothing.' Javeed deplored the fact that the recently upgraded gymkhana was now run as a modern gym while the gravel pit where he trained for years was hardly used anymore. For him this was another sign of the weakness and loss of strength that was the cause of the predicament of Muslims in India. Although liberal with his sons' behavior, Javeed had rather conservative ideas about family life and about how a respectable Muslim should behave. He spent most of his time out and about while his wife and daughters spent most of their time in the family home. Yet, Javeed was not a flamboyant man who loved attention and visibility. He was always impatient, straight to the point and preferred to meet people in his workplace or inside houses rather than in the street or the *chai* shop. None of his men dressed in the 'filmi' *dada*-style (sunglasses, leather jacket, etc.) which Javeed regarded as ridiculous and 'like Shah Rukh Khan', that is, men who dress up for the girls. Javeed was never impressed by the playboy style of Dawood Ibrahim, the famous expatriate gangster king of Bombay. He did admire Dawood for one thing though—his self-respect: 'We should all be like Dawood' he once told me 'we should respect ourselves'. He obviously preferred Haji Mastaan, the legendary smuggler king of the 1960s and 1970s since the latter had claimed that he had been reformed, and had styled himself as a melancholic and pious 'philosopher king' in the later part of his life.

Javeed's physical movements were quick and his bearing exuded a nervous energy and will power that made his men submit to every wish he had. When he moved around in the streets, or in his car, people would smile and show deference and respect. Many would also cast nervous glances in his direction as if they expected something bad or violent to happen by virtue of his mere presence. There was this indefinable aura around the man, a kind of 'dark energy', which undoubtedly had to do with a reputation that was heroic, menacing, and violent at the same time. His men were indeed known as brutal enforcers and debt collectors, I was told, but no-one had ever witnessed Javeed himself hurt anyone since he returned from prison. His reputation was established and had acquired a life of its own, based on rumors, whispers and stories.

His conduct during the riots in 1993 had improved and confirmed his standing as a fighter and defender of the neighborhood. Javeed and his men, including Junaid, had been awake night and day during those weeks. They had patrolled the streets and warded off several attacks by groups of men organized by the Shiv Sena. The most intense confrontations had taken place around a particular street with traditional *chawls*—some Hindu, others Muslim. 'We call this area Jammu and Kashmir' Javeed's brother told me. 'We were there, defending the Muslim side and we kept them out of our *mohalla*', he claimed. While many locals acknowledged these deeds, others pointed out that Javeed was weak because he was an enemy of the police. This was why he could do nothing to help ease the curfew imposed on the area for many days during the riots. Javeed had no clout with the police and it was only after a group of mothers had marched to the police station to demand milk and food after five days of curfew that the police had given in.

Javeed never spoke of that incident but never denied it either. For his reputation, the distance to the police was of utmost importance. The men who worked with the police as informers and 'helpers' were like women, he claimed, men without honor and self-respect. 'They are all *julahas*' he used to say, 'a Khan would never help the Shiv Sena police', as he always referred to the police force. Whether Javeed was forced to pay *hafta* to the police, like most other businessmen, was impossible to say but he carefully maintained the public image as a self-reliant man, an antithesis to the police, and therefore a law unto himself.

A few years before I met him he had joined the Samajwadi Party and was now chairing its local branch. He identified strongly with Mulayam Singh whose rhetoric and strong stance against Hindutva he admired. 'I am not anti-Hindu but I am against people who speak with sweetness and then stab you in the back....Congress, the BJP and also Janata Dal.....Thackeray is my enemy because he is against Muslims but you know what he stands for, he is direct (*sida*) and I respect that.'

Javeed was instrumental in getting Mulayam Singh to his area several times and the Samajwadis have done well among the Muslims in his locality. He was proud of his work and considered running for the post as Municipal Councillor in his ward. But something held him back and he was not so keen on campaigning, persuading people to give him their vote. Somehow I could not imagine this proud man humbly asking for votes from voters, pledging to serve the locality as most candidates do all the time. Javeed was used to getting his way, not asking for favors. I asked him whether he would stand in the future and he smiled and gave me an enigmatic answer that summed up his life and his experience: 'I know what visibility (*dikhna*) can bring.' In some ways this also summed up a broader sentiment of apprehension and angry patience among the Muslims in his locality.

5

Mohmedhusain
Words, Tabloids and the
Compulsions of the Ahl-e-Hadis

FARHANA IBRAHIM AND EDWARD SIMPSON

Mohmedhusain's visiting card lists his competences as tours, bird watching and anthropology. We both (authors) know him, in different ways, through anthropology, but have also learned to appreciate him for his gentle knowledge of his land, its beauties and mysteries, as well as of its flora and fauna. We have both employed him at different times over the last few years to assist with our research, and have both struggled as the boundaries between friendship and the demands of work have slowly dissolved. In part, we also got to know one another through him.

We had thought writing about Mohmedhusain would be a simple task because we both enjoy his company, are indebted to him, and have enjoyed days traveling with him through the vast landscapes of Kachchh, his home, in the westernmost part of Gujarat. However, the task proved to be far from simple and we now appreciate why so very few biographies are co-authored. The complexities of subjectivity, relationships and experience cloud the terrain of making certain statements with alacrity. We had imagined a character sketch and a number of illustrative anecdotes would serve as an introduction to Mohmedhusain's passion for language, newspapers and a particular brand of Islamic thought and practice. Preliminary drafts of this piece provoked lengthy and circuitous discussions about its future content and direction. It became clear to us that we knew him in quite different ways, had found different common grounds with both him and his family, and were both intimate with quite different aspects of his personality and interests. As our names loosely reflect, we took different genders, languages and histories into our relationships with Mohmedhusain. The reader will clearly see the consequences of this in the stories that follow.

Mohmedhusain is known to his family, friends and acquaintances simply as MB. He belongs to the large Muslim dyer and block printer Khatri community that is found throughout the towns and villages of Kachchh. MB lives, surrounded by extended family, in the provincial town of Bhuj, the geographical and administrative centre of Kachchh. The walled centre of the town, like many others in South Asia, has at its core a complex of royal palaces, the *darbar gadh*, itself encircled by a high wall. Outside the palace grounds lie the bazaar on one side and the residential localities all around in semi-concentric half circles. Residence was, and still is, dictated largely by caste, sectarian and occupational affiliations. Closest to the palace grounds lived those communities that have historically provided services to the royal courts, their shops close by in the bazaar area. The Muslim Khatris live fairly close to the palace grounds, in an area appropriately known as Khatri Chakla, the Kachchhi term for *chowk* or square, a mere toss of a stone from Danda Bazaar where family-run shops sell brightly coloured tie-dyed fabrics to admiring visitors and locals alike.

Around Khatri Chakla live a number of high-status Hindu castes. Inter-communal relations between these different communities and the Khatris have generally been affable, at least when measured against other parts of Gujarat—now infamous for religious polarization, and, especially, the widespread violence of 2002. The residents of Khatri Chakla and other nearby neighborhoods talk with pride of the centuries of relatively happy co-existence, of Muslim neighborhoods and Hindu ones, all nestled one within the other.

For MB, this pride, like the history of his neighborhood, is intimately related to the comings and goings of his family, their property acquisitions and the making and unmaking of religious and community buildings and institutions. The area is also literally inscribed with memories of his ancestors; both his father and grandfather were killed in accidents close to his house. His father lost his life to an exploding gas cylinder in his cycle workshop and his grandfather, similarly, met his end in a fire accident in a small shop commissioned by the then princely state of Kachchh to produce fire crackers. It was never far from the front of more stoical parts of

MB's mind that the same fate might await him: a random death in a random accident.

Like a great many government employees of his generation, MB took voluntary early retirement from his clerical position at a local branch of the Bank of India. Encouraged by the significant financial incentive, he was then 52, he looked forward to a sunny retired life, devoted to the pursuit of his wide-ranging hobbies. He imagined wandering, carefree, into the bazaars on Sunday to browse the second-hand book stalls in search of back issues of *National Geographic* and other glossy foreign-printed magazines. The pages of these publications allow him a privileged glimpse into the world writ large, and more specifically into the lives of the Hollywood actors and actresses, and the British royal family, especially, Princess Diana, who so intrigue him. Over the years, he had amassed a sizeable collection of press clippings and photographs of the glitterati which he preserves, quite lovingly, along with other similar treasures in an old trunk. He also imagined his retirement would bring with it some amateur study, reflecting his keen interest in foreign languages, the mores and graces of European, Israeli and Japanese societies, and trips out to the wildernesses of Kachchh to watch migratory flocks with the local ornithological club, 'The Pelicans'. With the lump sum of money he had received upon his retirement, life was just beginning to look up for him.

There is however no guarantee that life is fair or just; life has an uncanny knack of following its own designs in the face of the most carefully laid plans. On 26 January 2001, barely a month into MB's retirement, Kachchh was rocked by a powerful earthquake. Even in an area that has been at the receiving end of frequent seismically induced catastrophe, this time around, the pieces were harder to put together. Vast swathes of Bhuj were reduced to rubble. On that bitterly cold January morning in 2001, as MB was sitting on the floor of his house, writing a letter to one of his pen friends, the earthquake struck, and parts of his house came crashing down. His family, which at the time consisted of his wife, an unmarried daughter, two sons, a daughter–in-law and his beloved granddaughter, who was only a few months old, ran up to the roof of his two storey house and huddled together while other houses, shops and religious buildings tumbled all around them. When he looked up, all he could see was a fine mist of dust and cement. As the day wore on, the extent of the damage became apparent Trapped under the rubble, scores of people from his neighborhood had died. The families of his two brothers survived: He was grateful for that, even though his own beloved home, which he had built himself with a loan from the bank some years ago, and named 'Ashiyana' (shelter or nest), was badly damaged. The earthquake reordered his priorities, and, clearly, his retirement would now take on new meanings.

The earthquake was a catastrophic interloper in MB's plans, but it was accompanied by another less dramatic peril: the falling interest rates which were slowly eroding the value of his savings. He had worked as a guide to foreign tourists in the past, as a labor of love and to supplement his salary from the bank, but he now thought of taking it up more seriously as a much-needed source of income. Like many tourists, we also benefitted from his genuine, affable and honest nature. He shared with us the experience of previous travel in Kachchh, a wide network of familiar, familial and friendly contacts, a passion for natural history and an ability to gauge, with considerable accuracy, what people do not know and what it would please them to hear. Over the years, he had learned to represent his homeland in multiple ways to foreigners with varying constraints on their budget, time, intellectual capacities and interests. Admirable qualities for a guide—or an anthropologist in need of guidance—indeed!

However, MB now had to adopt a more mercenary approach; he had a house to repair and sons who needed help in rebuilding their business. The number of tourists visiting Bhuj was never very high and this flow was further reduced by the earthquake. Competition for relieving foreign visitors of their wealth is tough in Bhuj and handicraft producers, antique dealers and hoteliers come together in constantly shifting patterns of competitive allegiance and coalition. In this rather cut and thrust world, lies are told, discretionary payments made and hard bargains struck. MB is a poor liar, and often recapitulates under the slightest of pressures. He looks rather uncomfortable standing in the lobbies of some of Bhuj's more 'upmarket' hotels. He clearly dislikes talking about money and naming his price and he never seems to be at the forefront of the knowledge networks that allow his rivals to know who is coming, who is staying where and who wants what kind of tour or guidance. Simply, he is not as hard-nosed as other guides and frequently invites travellers to his home to eat his profits; he remembers many of those he works with and writes to some long after they have gone. His career in the bank may not have prepared him for the rigors of private enterprise, but he is aware of his limitations. He started to seek other work in the burgeoning charity and social work sector that sprang up in the aftermath of the earthquake. Without success, and disillusioned, he once said, in rather melancholy tones, 'I am in my fifties. I have not learned how to do anything other people value, or at least are willing to pay for.'

Trade and business has been the Kachchhis' forte from time immemorial, both Hindu as well as Muslim. Even today, migrant Kachchhis are known to make some of the shrewdest businesspeople, as evidenced in places such as Mumbai and beyond. In a society of traders and shopkeepers, MB, by taking work in a bank, had already aspired for a life beyond the obvious. Most of his Khatri brethren continue in their traditional business of cloth and dyeing. Local positions of authority are usually cornered by high-caste Hindus and it remains rather unusual for a Muslim to find himself in such government posts. As a young recruit to the bank, he worked initially in Gandhidham, a post-independence township about 50 kilometers east of Bhuj, built primarily for Sindhi migrants from what became Pakistan. Living away from home and the conservative influence of the family, he learned the ways of the world. He lived together with a number of other young working bachelors in a rented apartment, and it was here that he formed a series of lifelong friendships. In a relatively insular social world, where Kachchhis, and more so Muslims, socialize within their own caste and religious sets, MB is remarkable for having crossed that divide such a long time ago. Some of his closest friends are people who do not share his religion or worldview, but he visits them often, and, in his youth, went on long holidays with them to places as far away as Srinagar and Chennai.

Today, a middle-aged MB clearly enjoys his status of culture broker not just within his community but also beyond that. When people among the community need bureaucratic forms filled out, someone to put in a good word for them among the higher echelons of authority, or to present a sophisticated argument to significant authorities, it is but natural that they turn to him.

Edward and MB

I first met the clean-shaven, ambitiously spectacled and smartly dressed man who became known to me as MB in Bhuj during 2002. His fame and contacts had already enveloped me from working in other parts of Kachchh in previous years and, by 2002, I felt as if I already knew him. In contrast to Farhana's experience (below), the mutual celebration of religious ideas never became a prominent part of our relationship. He assumed instantly, and for the most part correctly, that as a European of a certain character I probably entertained some rather vague and non-committal notions about god and propriety. Although he knew that I had an interest in Islam in India, and that I had published some material on the topic, our discussions of Islam always felt clumsy, superficial and somewhat contrived. He also knew that I had published critical words on the actions and policies of the ruling BJP government in Gujarat; he had even less interest in cultivating or exploiting this potential aspect of our relationship.

There are many things I could write about MB that would lend humanity and depth to the portraiture of Muslims in India. However, I wish simply to recount two stories, which solely for the sake of convenience, I will call 'the story of the book club' and 'the story of the *Sun*'. These stories coax out two related aspects of MB's personality, his love of public order and regulation in his dealings with others on the one hand, and his personal flights of imagination in which rule and regulation (and the expectations local society had of him) are firmly demoted. The portrait of a Muslim I am thus able to outline is one of a man who treated me paternally, carefully and with measured respect; a portrait in which the hues and textures of religious value and practice stand in proportional relationship to the significance of friendship between men of different backgrounds.

Way back then, in 2002, he kindly showed me the nooks and crannies of post-earthquake Bhuj with the sensitivity of an insider and did his best to introduce me to some of the town's notables. We traversed rough terrain by motorbike in the north of Kachchh, got the bike stuck in sand and grew increasingly dehydrated in the desert conditions during Ramadan. Looking back on those times, however irritating we may have found one another then, I feel a strong sense of privilege to have shared these experiences with MB.

MB is well-versed in English, something at which he works assiduously, by reading, painstakingly, anything that comes his way through passing tourists, as well as by looking at the English-language newspaper every day. Frequently, after dinner (and there have been lots of those), I would sit with him and discuss the English language as an expansive collection of words, idioms and phrases. He was especially interested in dictionaries and we talked of the merits of various styles and publishing houses, the kinds of definitions provided and the pertinence of the kinds of usage (colloquial and otherwise) provided as example. At the time, MB had two rather tatty, over-thumbed dictionaries, one of which had lost its cover. He knew by heart the lists of weights and measures, proper nouns and country capitals found within the back cover of one of the volumes. For the last few years, he had been mulling over the possibility of buying a new dictionary: his vocabulary had outgrown the ones he owned. He had looked around in Bhuj, but his knowledge was not tested by the Gujarati-English-Gujarati or Hindi-English dictionaries that were available locally. He had asked a few people in Bombay to see what was available there, but the editions they discovered from international publishing houses were too expensive.

His interest in words often astonished me; while I struggled with Gujarati, I could only marvel at how he managed to remember new vocabulary so easily, let alone how he could use it so proficiently and sensitively. He only needed to hear new words once from the television or from tourists, or to read a new word in the *Indian Express*. He would remember it, check it in his dictionaries and it was his to possess, use and impress others with.

One morning in the spring of 2004, he called me at home in Bhuj, saying he had to urgently discuss the topic of dictionaries. He had received a glossy brochure from a British book club. In return for joining the club, he was being offered a free two-volume edition of the *Shorter Oxford English Dictionary*. The dictionaries had attractive and scholarly-looking black leather binding and came with the added incentive of a free pen. In addition to such gifts, which could be kept without any further obligation, the club was also offering a further set of reference books with the proviso that they receive orders for at least four books from their regular catalogue within a year. Before arriving at my house, he had studied the brochure diligently. He knew the small print by heart and had thought hard about the terms and conditions. He was visibly excited about the opportunity of getting a hefty dictionary delivered to his door without parting with any of his own money.

He passed the brochure to me, asking me to read it. He wanted to know whether the company was reputable, why they were offering so many free gifts and if there were any snags he could not foresee. He was already two steps ahead of me and had thought of a solution to all of the problems I raised. The company had a distribution warehouse in Chennai so there would not be the problem of international postage costs. They sent him a brochure with his name already embossed on the cover so they already considered him to be a suitable customer. I told him that the books offered in the catalogue would be expensive and that he might not be interested in spending his money on the titles they offered. He had already considered that and told me that the dictionaries were his to keep, along with the pen. He could return the other volumes and be free of his obligation to order further books from the catalogue. The point here for him was that he would gain a beautiful dictionary for the cost of returning the extra five books. The only problem he could foresee was that the Indian postal service might take longer than the 15 days necessary to return the other volumes. But he would get proof of postage so if any action was taken against him he would have some evidence of the fact that he was not at fault.

MB's attention to detail, perhaps from his banking years, is reflected in the lengths to which he is prepared to go in pursuit of his interests and his painstaking attention to procedure, if not to say in his cunning. I had strongly advised MB not to get sucked into the strange world of book clubs, which, in my experience, derive their profits from deliberate maladministration, intimidation, under-staffed call centers and a dependency on the slovenly and lackadaisical attitude of their customers. MB however had a rather different view of the book club's offer. For him, there were rules and regulations that were to be followed to the letter, and, besides, he questioned, 'when rules fail, or a misunderstanding occurs, what power can a foreign book club have over me here?' Simply, if the world was populated by people as diligent as MB, such book clubs could not survive; their alluring introductory offers would cost them too dearly.

The allure was greater than the simple offer of free dictionaries; the foreign nature of the book club and the bold prose of its publicity material had also hooked him. Such interests were by no means confined to books or to the study of language. His fascination with the British royals long predates Princess Diana's association with Dodi Al Fayed, and, over the years, MB has amassed a substantial archive of clippings recalling the life of the Princess. His interest extends to all of the royal family, their antics, love affairs, charity work and study. He is aware that British tabloid newspapers carry substantial coverage of royal events and other kinds of celebrity gossip. He had heard mention of a newspaper called the *Sun* and wanted a copy to read. I was not keen on buying it for him; and told him that I did not think it suitable, but he insisted, perhaps rightly objecting to my attempts at censure. I arranged for one to be sent from England, along with a copy of its main rival, the slightly left-of-center *Daily Mirror*. The newspapers instantly looked out of place in his house, their names emblazoned in distinctive red ink (they are known as 'Red Tops' in the trade in England), followed by bold headlines and revealing pictures of scantily clad celebrities. These papers are known for their glib (some might say concise) coverage of the news and their revelations about the sex lives of the rich and famous. I placed them on the couch in his living room. Something stopped him from picking them up straight away, an act that would certainly have drawn inquisitive questions from other members of his family; perhaps other guests arrived or we had to go out, I no longer remember, but then the newspapers remained unread. I met him a week later and asked him what he thought of the read. He smiled, an unusual and conspiratorial smile, saying that they were unsuitable for his house, which receives a steady flow of guests, and had put them upstairs in his office amid other treasures for private perusal.

To my mind, the story of the book club and the story of the *Sun* speak of different but complementary aspects of MB's character. The story of the book club reveals his easy relationship with rules and clearly defined procedures (this may also explain MB's attraction to certain religious ideas which Farhana touches on in what follows); this aspect of his character is concerned primarily with how he regulates his daily life, and his relationships with authority, finance, and, as I have implied, perhaps his public relationship with Islam and matters of religious belief and practice. The story of the *Sun* reveals something quite different: MB's private flights of fancy, in which locality and rules no longer matter, a world where he is free to have imagined relationships with Princesses and words.

MB knows a lot of things about the world that most people living around him have no idea about. His flights of fancy take him into imagined spaces that are difficult to reconcile with the daily life and public morality of Khatri Chakla. By policing the availability of his acquisitions, written mostly as they are in a language inaccessible to many of those around him, he has created a unique mental niche, physically expressed in his office, and exemplified by his trunk of treasures. The niche allows him to transcend the material and cultural demands of his immediate social life; here, anything is possible, the strictures of space, class, religion and gender collapse under the scrutiny of his imagination.

Farhana and MB

When I first met him in 2001, as an anthropologist looking for someone to help me learn the Kachchhi language, MB and his family were still recovering from the earthquake, living in a small room on the outskirts of Bhuj. Despite his exposure to and interest in the worlds of *National Geographic* and foreign tourism, anthropology was a new field for him. The following year, I returned to Kachchh for an extended period of fieldwork in 2002–3, and recruited him as a research assistant. By this time, anthropology had made it onto his freshly-printed glossy visiting card. As Edward's narrative highlighted, MB can be highly experimental with ideas and experiences that enable him to transcend the humdrum daily pattern of life in Khatri Chakla. During the year that I lived in Kachchh, he opened his home and worlds to me, and took a keen and active interest in my own research agenda. His enormous network of friends and associates enabled me to develop my own web of local acquaintances early on in my fieldwork and this is something that was to be a valuable asset. Over time, he became much more than a research assistant in the strict sense of the term. His family had become my surrogate family and he became a watchful father figure for me. From discussing local politics and religion, to nature, tourism and anthropology to accompanying me to the local bazaar in my early days to choose a pair of silver anklets (*de rigueur* for any woman who wants to be taken seriously locally!), he was always there as facilitator and friend. Despite this, MB is keenly aware of the material benefits to be had as culture broker and has few qualms about furthering his list of personal contacts by any possible means. Undoubtedly, I also added to his local prestige and standing that went far beyond any financial remuneration I offered him for his services. However, I was not the much coveted foreign tourist, whose acquaintance he remained ever keen to snatch from other potential rivals in the game. This adoration of the foreign tourist is not unusual, especially when they bring the possibility of earning some quick money as well as access to the more seductive aspects of 'Western culture', as Edward's anecdotes show, and I would tease him about this often. In the course of his interaction with me, I have reason to believe that he laid aside his more materialistic motivations in taking people under his wing.

His family saw me as a woman with part Muslim parentage, and some of them felt responsible for what I suspect they saw as my spiritual well-being. His wife, somewhat shrewder, sharper, and altogether more street-smart than MB, would constantly admonish me on the numerous days I would spend sitting around the Khatri household, learning to navigate my way around Kachchhi Muslim social worlds. Why don't you say your *namaz* (prayers); why haven't you started reading the Quran; why aren't you married? Or, calling me into the kitchen where she would be squatting with her daughter before the small kerosene stove churning out perfect round *rotla*s, come let's see whether you can cook at least! I felt I failed all of her tests for me, and felt miserable in my early days. MB would, significantly stay aloof from all these discussions. On occasion, prompted by his wife, he might say something about the 'moral' duty of all Muslims as he interpreted it, but always in our discussions, and at times violent arguments, he abstained from commenting on my own lack of proper moral, Islamic anchor, as his wife might have put it.

About six weeks into my fieldwork, I went along with him to a local *urs*. These are annual commemorations of the death of a saint (*pir*) at the relevant shrine (*dargah*). This particular *urs* was in honor of a saint whose tomb lay in a village some 13 kilometers from Bhuj. I was eager to meet people here and to perhaps identify this village as one of the key sites for my ethnography. From the point of view of my research question, this *urs* was thus an important one and I had forewarned MB of this. MB and I arrived at the village in the late afternoon, ahead of the festivities which would commence in the evening. As soon as we walked into the relevant hamlet we were greeted by a group of young girls and women, sitting around a huge pile of garlic which they were peeling in preparation for the feast that was to be cooked later. Large cooking pots were being readied for the occasion as well. This was for the preparation of the ritual meal or *niaz* that would be shared by all the devotees later in the evening. *Niaz* as ritual meal entails the communal sharing of the charisma (*barakat*). As devotees come together to worship at the shrine, they share in the *barakat* of the saint both in their individual communion with the saint as well as in the communal celebration of community. This occurs through sharing the food consecrated by *barakat*.

Once the ritual celebrations were over, we waited for the food to be prepared before we could leave. Night was falling steadily and we broke up into groups of men and women, scattered throughout the village. MB and I had missed the last bus back into Bhuj and were promised a ride back by the party of musicians who had been invited to play at the shrine. It seemed like an eternity had passed before one of the women of this group came up to me and advised me to tell my companion to go eat with the men, following which the women could eat and then we would leave for Bhuj. Relieved, I went to convey the message to him. I found him sitting outside, all by himself, maintaining a steady distance from the men whose group he had been a part of until only a short while ago. Surprised, I asked him why he wasn't eating as it was late and he must be hungry. He replied that he would not eat, that I could if I wished, but he refused to do so. I was surprised and frustrated, for he was usually of a very social disposition and would strike up friendships wherever we went. This time he was clearly uncomfortable, possibly even offended. I was torn between taking his side to not antagonize him further and the knowledge that refusing to eat would also jeopardize my future relations in a village that I hoped would become a key research site. I decided to abstain from the meal citing the fact that I did not eat meat, which was true. Our presence in the village, which had until then been largely unquestioned, suddenly became the focus of hostile attention. People came up to us suspiciously demanding to know who we were, what caste we belonged to. To have come all this way to the *urs*, participated in the ritual, stayed late into the night and then refused to eat was to make a statement of the most anti-social kind. For the next few visits back to this village, we were always referred to as the people who did not eat at the *urs*.

I was furious with him for, as I saw it, having put me in this predicament, of knowingly threatening my initial contact with an important set of informants, for creating an uncomfortable situation without explanation. Why had he refused to participate in something that forms one of the most basic social bonds between people, I demanded to know. I had known from earlier occasions that despite the rigid codes that governed inter-caste and religious norms of eating together, he had no problems accepting food or water from strangers, from Hindus and Jains, and here he was with a group of fellow Muslims, refusing to eat. His response was simple and straightforward: he refused to eat food cooked in the name of anyone other than Allah. Food cooked at a shrine, invoking the name of the saint instead of Allah constituted nothing short of blasphemy and he was going to have no part of that.

Even as I came to learn this about MB, I was curious to know what made him sit through that *urs*, in silent defiance. I realized in the days that followed that he was not about to bring up the issue with me either. We talked about the event over many weeks. Although used to taking tourists around Kachchh, MB had not really been an anthropologists' assistant until now, and the differences were only gradually dawning upon him as they were becoming apparent to me. Unlike all of our previous field trips until that day, I was in charge of the situation for the first time. In the past, MB would escort me to villages that were known to him, either through the tourist circuit, or because he had a friend or a relative there. In that regard, it was just like any other tourist excursion, as he showed off aspects of his ancestral land to me, pointing out bits of history, geography and society that was a welcome introduction to Kachchh for me. It would not be an exaggeration to say that I owe much of what I know about Kachchh to him. He would come to my house armed with a detailed road map and poring over it, would announce our itinerary for the day. I followed gratefully, for as a relative stranger to the area, I was happy to wander about everywhere. Gradually, as my own contacts strengthened, I would take charge, calling up MB to tell him which day we would go where and what we would do. It would be churlish to deny that he enjoyed these excursions any less than the ones he was directing, for above all, MB is animated by a sense of adventure, of the unknown.

On the *urs* in question, MB stayed, simply because I had wanted to. He would have liked to have taken the last bus back into town, but as we had both inadvertently missed it, he had no option but to stay the course. Once he made a personal commitment to me, he was not going to go back on his word. This is not to say that he would always act with this selfless spirit. However, as I have tried to point out in this piece, his attitude toward me was always rather protective. Blurring the divide between tourist and anthropologist in his mind, he was not about to abandon me.

This incident was a clear turning point in my fieldwork. The categories 'Islam' and 'Muslim', were sites of intense contestation and debate. I also realized in this moment that my research assistant shared an interpretation of Islam that was as purist as any fundamentalist I might have encountered. For someone so conversant and at ease with the idea of difference, his avid interest in things beyond his own lived experience, he was remarkably quick to dismiss as un-Islamic those beliefs and practices that did not accord with his own experience.

In Kachchh, the Barelwi, Ahl-e-Hadis, the Tablighi Jama'at and others, Islamic movements with differing interpretations of orthodoxy, legal legitimacy and ritual practices, compete for the attention and patronage of the Muslim population. Generally, non-Muslim populations have very little idea of the debates Muslims are having about religious practices or how different reformist currents are associated with particular mosques, caste groups or areas of the town. Although couched in different terms, in many ways these debates are not so dissimilar from long-running conversations within Jain and some Hindu communities about religious propriety and practice.

These movements are not limited to South Asia, and are part of a global call for Islamic reform and revivalism. In India, however, they date back to the late nineteenth century when scholars have identified the decline of the

Mughal Empire and associated loss of Muslim prestige in North India as the precipitating cause for these revival movements within Islam. It was at this time that the main reformist currents began to debate within themselves the contours of what Islam should be. The Tablighi Jamaat, Ahl-e-Hadis, and Deobandi were the main custodians of an orthodoxy, modeled often on the contemporary Wahhabi of Arabia or Salafi of East Africa and beyond. They differ in minute details, but are by and large, all opposed to Sufi practices, shrine visitations and so on. The Ahl-e-Hadis is seen as the most strict of the lot, going by the letter of the *hadith*, or Prophetic practice. In Kachchh, people frequently assert that they are Wahhabi, by which they really mean Ahl-e-Hadis, for there is no real Wahhabi following in the area.

As a self-professed member of the Ahl-e-Hadis, MB would rarely miss out on even one of the prescribed five daily prayers, and this with scant attention to where we happened to be. He and I traveled by bus to some of the remotest villages in northern Kachchh, just south of the Great Rann, poorly serviced by bus routes. For someone otherwise so attentive to my comfort and security, when he had to go to pray, he simply had to go and he would have few qualms about leaving me in the midst of an alien bazaar, at a stranger's house, or even just standing by a roadside tea stall, while he fulfilled his religious obligations. No matter if this zealous adherence to the letter of the *hadith* meant that we might miss the sole bus back into town! Predictably, this led to a certain amount of conflict between the two of us especially when he announced to me that he would rather not go out on a field trip on a Friday, in order to fulfill his religious duties. Every Friday is like Id, he informed me sombrely one day, and the *hadith* state that we should aspire to the same degree of piety every Friday as we would on Id. His own purism did not translate into a proselytizing zeal however, and he was happy to leave other people to their own devices as long as he could uphold his own. Within his own extended family, he was the only one who demonstrated this outlook. Of all the extended time I spent in his home, I rarely saw others pray as often as he did. Each Friday he would exhort his sons to come to the mosque for the noon prayer, and when they resisted, he just resigned himself to going alone, saying he would not force people to do things his way.

Why then, did he put up with an anthropologist who insisted on returning time and again to shrines and feasts cooked in the name of obscure saints? At no point in our research endeavor, did he ever rebuke me or decline from attendance, even though he was steadfast about maintaining his own ideological stance. Thus, he would enter the *dargah* space, head appropriately covered with a scarf or handkerchief, but would not bow his head. That was reserved for Allah.

Towards Rapprochement

The Government of India's Prevention of Terrorism Act of 2002 outlines strict measures to be taken against individuals and organizations suspected of engaging in anti-national activities. Unusually, the legislation also names a number of terrorist organizations which include the Lashkar-e-Taiba (Army of the Pure) and the Pasban-e-Ahle Hadis. These organizations, based in Pakistan, engage in party politics and seminary education. They have also been linked to acts of terrorism in India, including the bombing of the Indian Parliament buildings in 2002. However, the media in India and overseas has been far less accurate when describing these groups' affiliations, interests and networks in India. As a result, public perceptions and understandings of the differences between political organizations and religiously inspired movements have become blurred. The Lashkar-e-Taiba, for example, has often been associated with the Ahl-e-Hadis 'sect'. Some newspapers have suggested the Ahl-e-Hadis is the religious front for the Lashkar-e-Taiba. Such simplifications, which tar all followers of a particular religious organization with the same politicized brush, are harmful to the general perception of Islam in South Asia but are also hurtful to many Muslims who simply see religion as a question of faith rather than as an explicitly politicized activity.

MB is not explicitly politicized but he is a purist, and, importantly, for him this is a question of faith and religious authenticity, a mark of progress and rationality rather than of bigotry or intolerance. So where did MB get this knowledge of a 'pure' Islam? He talks of how his father converted to the Ahl-e-Hadis doctrine when MB was still a young boy. One of his family's tenants in the Khatri Chakla area was an early Ahl-e-Hadis 'convert', and late at night when the men would sit around in the neighborhood square, drinking tea and talking, as they still do, he would talk of religion and the superstitious ways of the Kachchhi Muslims. It was then that MB's father gradually moved over to the Ahl-e-Hadis. MB talks of his mother being a compulsive believer in saints and their miracles. His father let her do as she pleased, MB recalls. In fact as a small child, MB was made to enact his mother's vows on his behalf. As he used to suffer much from sore throats and other minor ailments, his mother would keep vows (*mannat*s) on his behalf. One time, MB recalled with a sheepish smile, he sat up for 40 nights in a row at a *dargah* in Bhuj because his mother had promised the saint she would send her son to him if he cured him of his childhood sicknesses. As an active participant in these rituals as a child, he recalls how he gradually came to 'see the light'. In the heart of the old city, close to Khatri Chakla, lies a mosque where he came as a college student to listen to the late night *takrir*s of a well-known *maulana* of the Tablighi Jamaat. Most mosques belong to one or another denomination and even now MBs fanaticism is tempered, as he says he does not mind going to mosques that are non-Ahl-e-Hadis. 'How can you call me a fundamentalist', he asks with a smile, 'I am so open to all, I go to every mosque. The others are the ones who give us a bad name always. They do not go to Ahl-e-Hadis mosques but have you ever seen me spurn another's mosque? It is the abode of Allah, whoever runs it, and I have no argument with them.' For MB, the discourse of progress is important in a day and age when he sees the Hindus so well organized with their own religious, cultural and political organizations. He may be a humanist and even with a profound interest in the profane, even bordering on the *risqué*, but religion is for him a serious matter of being bound to particular rules, and, more importantly of being 'modern' and 'rational'.

Aisha, the *Madrasah* Teacher

PATRICIA JEFFERY, ROGER JEFFERY AND CRAIG JEFFREY[1]

A isha's classroom was at one end of the veranda onto which all the other girls' classrooms opened, upstairs and out of sight of the mosque and the boys' classrooms surrounding the *madrasah* courtyard. The classroom was some three meters square, and its dingy paintwork and borrowed light made it hard to adjust to the dimness after the glaring sunlight outside. Aisha was sitting on rush matting behind a low bench, wearing a full-length black robe, with long sleeves buttoned at the cuffs. She had wrapped a large black *dupatta* with black lace edging around her shoulders and over her head twice, securing it round her chin and temples so that only her face was

[1] We thank the Economic and Social Research Council (Grant R000238495), the Ford Foundation and the Royal Geographical Society for funding aspects of this research on secondary education, and the Institute of Economic Growth, New Delhi, for our attachment in 2000–2002. We were in Bijnor October–April 2000–2001 and October–April 2001–2. We are grateful to our research assistants, Swaleha Begum, Shaila Rais, Chhaya Sharma and Manjula Sharma, to the people of our two study villages, and to the schoolteachers, *madrasah* staff and others who so readily answered our questions. For more on *madrasah*s in Bijnor, see P. Jeffery, R. Jeffery and C. Jeffery, 2004, 'Islamisation, Gentrification and Domestication: "A Girls' Islamic Course" and Rural Muslims in Western Uttar Pradesh', *Modern Asian Studies*, 38, pp. 1–54, P. Jeffery, R. Jeffery and C. Jeffery, 2005, 'The Mother's Lap and the Civilising Mission: *Madrasah* Education and Rural Muslim Girls in Western Uttar Pradesh', in Zoya Hasan and Ritu Menon (eds.), *In a Minority: Essays on Muslim Women in India*, New Delhi: Oxford University Press and New Jersey: Rutgers University Press, pp. 108–48, and P. Jeffery, R. Jeffery and C. Jeffery, 2007, 'Investing in the Future: Education in the Social and Cultural Reproduction of Muslims in UP', in Mushirul Hasan (ed.), *Living with Secularism: The Destiny of India's Muslims*, New Delhi: Manohar, pp. 63–89; for general accounts of the educational profile in UP, and especially the gender disparities, see

showing. It was about 2 p.m. and she had just finished teaching for the day. She invited us—Patricia and Manjula—to sit down on the matting in front of her desk.[2]

Aisha's pupils—half a dozen teenage girls only a few years her junior—had been packing up, but not to her satisfaction. She summoned them back. 'What is this, that the things were placed in this fashion? Khuda [God] has given you good sense, na? What will the big master say if he sees this? From the first day I've been saying that things should be placed properly—but no one remembers!' Suitably shamed, one of the girls started sorting out the mats, but was hampered by the books she was holding. When Aisha told her to use both hands, the girl put the books on the floor, only to be told to put them tidily into the niche in the wall and to pile the matting on top of the benches to prevent them becoming wet if the water pump on the roof leaked onto them. But the benches had been thrown together in such a way that one was tilting and partially resting on another—so the more mats that were put on top, the more precarious the pile became. When it was eventually sorted out, Aisha grinned and shrugged her shoulders in a gesture of mock despair.

Our initial efforts to contact Aisha had not looked propitious. When we first phoned the *madrasah*, we were told there was no one of that name. The second time we phoned, we were not allowed to speak to her, but were told

J. Drèze and H. Gazdar, 1997, 'Uttar Pradesh: The Burden of Inertia', in J. Drèze and A. Sen (eds.), *Indian Development: Selected Regional Perspectives*, New Delhi: Oxford University Press, pp. 33–128; J. Drèze and A. Sen, 2002, *India: Development and Participation*, New Delhi: Oxford University Press, pp. 143–88, 229–73; M. Karlekar, 2000, 'Girls' Access to Schooling: An Assessment', in R. Wazir (ed.), *The Gender Gap in Basic Education: NGOs as Change Agents*, New Delhi: Sage Publications, pp. 80–114; L. McDougall, 2000, 'Gender Gap in Literacy in Uttar Pradesh: Questions for Decentralised Educational Planning', *Economic and Political Weekly*, 35 (19), pp. 1649–658; U. Nayar, 2001, 'Education of Girls in India: An Assessment', in R. Govinda (ed.), *India Education Report: A Profile of Basic Education*, New Delhi: National Institute of Educational Planning and Administration, pp. 35–46; R. Srivastava, 2001, 'Access to Basic Education in Rural Uttar Pradesh', in A. Vaidyanathan and P.R. Gopinathan Nair (eds.), *Elementary Education in Rural India: A Grassroots View*, New Delhi: Sage Publications, pp. 257–319; The Probe Team, 1999, *Public Report on Basic Education in India*, New Delhi: Oxford University Press.

[2] Manjula Sharma took detailed notes of our conversations to write up later. Patricia translated these accounts into English, trying to capture both the content and the spirit of what Aisha said. The English words and phrases that she used have been rendered in italics here. We have not included Aisha's comments on teaching and how children learn. Aisha is a pseudonym.

to come in person to arrange a meeting. But when we arrived at the *madrasah*, the principal greeted us with his usual cheery grin and a wave—and told us to go and find her. Aisha explained that many of the staff did not know she was there because she practiced *parda* in front of her male colleagues. When she was called to speak to us on the phone, she had asked the principal what to do and he told her to return to her classroom. 'Basically,' she said, 'talking to anyone like that isn't right for women. But now I've met you *face-to-face.* Now there's no problem.' And she smiled broadly. Patricia explained our research and said we would like to talk to her. She agreed enthusiastically to a meeting the next day—adding the somewhat chilling rider 'if Allah wills it, certainly, provided that death does not intervene'—and she gave us her home telephone number so that we could contact her directly if necessary.

Aisha turned out to be a thoughtful and captivating speaker, with a mischievous sense of humor. She would look down after our questions to reflect for a moment, or stop to readjust her *dupattâ* (which kept slithering out of place)—and then raise her eyes and speak with such verve that her words tumbled one after another. She peppered her comments with laughter and garnished her Urdu with 'if Allah wills' [*insha-llah*] and 'all the praises are for Allah' [*alhamdulillah*] in Arabic—as well as English vocabulary and turns of phrase. We were spellbound.

✳   ✳   ✳

Aisha's father was originally from Qaziwala, a village close to Begawala—where the *madrasah* was—and some 5 kilometers from Bijnor, a district town in western Uttar Pradesh. He is a *nai* (or Barber, one of the lower Muslim castes). He has not lived in Qaziwala regularly for many years: like several other *nai*s from Qaziwala, he runs a 'cosmetic shop' in Srinagar, Kashmir, more than 600 kilometers northwest from his home. Thus Aisha had spent her childhood in Kashmir, punctuated by several lengthy visits to Qaziwala. She attended a private primary school in Srinagar for some years, studied Urdu and the Quran Sharif at the Begawala *madrasah*, attended an Islamiyya school in Srinagar in which 'history, civics, math, English, Hindi—all kinds of education were given' and subsequently went to an English-medium private school, where she studied until she was about 13 years old.

Then, in 1995, she began studying at a girls boarding *madrasah* in Gujarat, some 1,500 kilometers south of Kashmir. She studied there for seven years and graduated as *Alima Fazila,* having added Arabic and Farsi (Persian) to her repertoire. Since she already knew English and some Arabic, Aisha explained, she was admitted directly into the second year of the seven-year curriculum. She did not have any special difficulties, though she had to work somewhat harder to learn Arabic. But in any case, 'the [watching] eye is Allah's, so that no difficulties will come.' But for having to waste (as she put it) one year because of illness, she would have completed her studies within six years: 'My studies were easy. I had already read the Quran Sharif and I knew English too. So there was no difficulty. ... After this course, a girl comes out with *Alima Fazila.* An *alima* is a learned woman, and *fazila* means someone who has put *fazilat* [excellence] into their learning.' Aisha explained that the name of the *madrasah*—Madrasah Islahul Banat—means for the good nurturing of girls. There were over 350 students, from small girls to young women, and they came from all over the world. Only girls who were already somewhat educated were admitted. 'There was a *rule* that every girl will speak either Urdu or Arabic,' Aisha explained. 'No other language would be spoken. If girls were to speak in their own languages, then it could come into the minds of other girls that maybe bad things are being said about them.'

How had her father heard about the *madrasah*? Aisha explained that he was a *Jamaati*—involved in the Islamic missionary or *tablighi* movement—and thus he knows many people: 'Those people told him about the *madrasah* in Gujarat. They told him it's a very big *madrasah* and alongside Urdu and Farsi they teach *typing* and *sewing.* And there's a *hostel.* In the *hostel* there are all kinds of conveniences for the girls. Food is provided from there, the bed, covers, blankets. They used to make every necessary thing available. There's also a *course* for *cooking.* The girls can learn all that work.' It had been her parents' wish that she study to become *Alima Fazila*: 'The atmosphere of our home was very different. There was a prayerful atmosphere in the house—an atmosphere of living according to one's religion and one's faith. Everyone wanted me to study and become an *Alima.*' Was this also what she herself had wanted? Aisha said, 'No—my own desires were different. When I was studying in school, my own desire was to study English and Hindi thoroughly. But when I was sent to the *madrasah,* my desires changed.'

Surely her father's opinions were quite unusual? Aisha said her father's *nature* had been different from the outset. 'Even within our wider family, the views of the people in my household are different from everyone else's. My parents wanted to educate me, but the people of the wider family created a lot of obstacles. They used to say, "Don't educate the girl so much, don't let her go outside [to Gujarat]." Abbu used to say, "This is my daughter and I want her to study and make progress." When I was in the *hostel*, these relatives used to ask my *Daddy*, "Why have you sent your girl to another place? If you can't take care of her, then send her to us and we'll care for her." Abba used to say that I was his daughter and he had no worries about looking after me, but he wanted to make me into something.' Her father, she said, 'has great enthusiasm for education'.

But many people consider that girls should not be educated—presumably Aisha did not agree? Aisha nodded enthusiastically. 'The big-big people, the *alim fazil* people have said that everyone has the same mind, that Allah has given everyone the same mind. It's up to you how much attention you pay. The mind grows by as much as you pay attention and the one who doesn't pay attention remains behind. It all *depends* on hard work. The mind of one who works hard will become strong. The mind of one who does not remains deficient. People who talk, many people, say that a woman's mind is behind her neck, that women are less than men, that women cannot compete with men, that they cannot rival men. This matter is true: a woman cannot be the equal of men. In some matters, men are more advanced than women. But this cannot be said in the matter of intelligence. A woman has the same mind as a man. She, too, understands many things and she can give advice. It is correct that a man goes outside and is more educated than a woman. But if he is about to do some task, if he is thinking of doing some *business*, and if he mentions this to his wife, then she, too, can give some advice which even her husband may not know. A woman and a man are for making good each other's shortcomings. If the man is ahead on some matter, then the woman can be ahead of him on another. Allah has given one thing to the man, so he has given another to the woman.'

Many people in Qaziwala would not agree with this—so how did they respond to her continuing to study? Was there a lot of gossip? 'Yes,' said Aisha with a grin, 'People talked. They also said things about me—but we didn't heed them. Things were said about my cousin and she had to leave her studies, because the people of her house didn't let her study further. I was also challenged, but my Abbu didn't heed anything. My cousin has remained just able to read Quran Sharif and Urdu. But my household is different. Allah-tala sent us [to this world], having made us different from everyone else, all the praises are for Allah. That's why I studied. My older sister wanted to study, but our paternal grandfather and our father's brothers, everyone said things and so her education was stopped.... Everyone pressurized my father, and so my sister was married at only 16 years of age to our paternal uncle's son. My grandfather said this should happen and so my father did it. But my father sent me outside. If the bamboo [*bans*] is not there, the flute [*bansuri*] will not play: he thought, *na*, that neither would anyone see me nor would anyone cause me to be married quickly. My father doesn't want me to remain dependent on anyone. He wants me to become something capable, so that if any bad time comes, I won't have to look helplessly at anyone's face. In the village we lived according to our own reckoning, in Kashmir we also lived according to our own reckoning. We didn't become dyed by other people's color.'

Her father's determination did not come cheap, though. Whilst Aisha was studying in the *madrasah,* he paid out Rs 8,000 per annum, a sum that covered everything in addition to the teaching—food and drink, living, clothes, bedding and covers, pillow cases and blankets. Had he been unable to pay this much, though, the fees would have been reduced: the Principal is from South Africa and he and his seven brothers are all wealthy. The *madrasah* is built on his land, on which the grains, legumes, vegetables and sugar eaten in the *madrasah* are also grown.

❋ ❋ ❋

When Patricia asked about life in Madrasah Islahul Banat, Aisha began chattering vivaciously at breakneck speed, her eyes glinting with enthusiasm, and pausing only to laugh or think about some of our additional questions. But she needed little prompting.

The girls slept in large *halls*: 'Every girl's bed was separate and all her things were separate. Two girls couldn't sleep together. Even two girls sleeping on one bed was forbidden. Everything was set in order.' Each girl had a *cupboard* with numerous compartments for her possessions. And the girls could wash their clothes and bedding in the laundry on one of their free days. The *madrasah* uniform was their *burqa*, which was green and underneath which they could wear clothes of any color, Aisha explained. But surely they only wore the *burqa* when they went outside? "We didn't go outside!" Aisha said emphatically, but with a grin. "We wore the *burqa* inside the *madrasah*. The *burqa* was long, like a loose cloak and made from a piece of circular material, with a hole that was suitable for letting the face out. You put your face through and then secured it at the throat, and then you spread it around you before sitting down' [she gestured all this as she was talking] 'and there were no sleeves. All the girls had to wear it, from the nursery class right up to the big girls.... And there was a *canteen* [general shop]. Any girl could go to the *canteen* after 2 p.m. and buy whatever she needed. Whatever food and drink items she wanted, she could buy, *juice*, *bread* and so on.... Everything that was needed was there. There was also a doctor. He was a *gents*, and there was also his dispensary. He was a good and expert doctor. If any girl's health became bad, she'd be taken to the dispensary.'

Did the *madrasah* monitor the pupils' visitors closely, as happens in other girls' *madrasahs*? Aisha said her family members visited her. They also telephoned from Kashmir to check how she was, but 'the students didn't talk on the telephone. Our Principal-*saheb* himself would talk on the phone and afterwards he used to tell us that a phone call had come from home, there are these-these matters, they said such-and-such. There are so many children, and they couldn't all be called time and again to the telephone.... My parents and my uncle could visit me, my real uncle. But not my cousins or anyone else. My real brother could visit me. At the time of admission, we were asked who would visit and what they looked like. "What, is there a beard? Is there a moustache? How tall are they?" They used to get this kind of knowledge. If someone visited us, we'd be shown them from a distance and asked if we recognized them, who is this? If we did, then they allowed us to meet them. It wasn't possible to meet just anyone who came.'

Just then, we heard one of the male teachers at the *madrasah* approaching. Aisha stiffened, on guard. From outside the classroom door he asked if we also wanted to interview him. Bemused, Patricia raised an eyebrow in Aisha's direction. She caught the glance and suppressed a giggle. Then he put his head around the door. Aisha was almost caught out—but swiftly hid her face with her *dupatta*, leaving just her eyes showing. She turned her eyes away from the doorway, and he backed out. Aisha uncovered her face again—and pouted at us, annoyed at his intrusion. For a while, he continued to hover outside the classroom, and Aisha kept adjusting the window shutters to prevent him from seeing inside. But he soon tired of our monosyllabic responses and wandered back downstairs.

Aisha paused for a moment and then resumed her story: the girls at Madrasah Islahul Banat, she said, spent their waking hours studying, taught by a *muallim saheb*. Did she really mean a male teacher? Were there no women teachers there? Aisha nodded. So did the men sit in front of the girls to teach? 'They did not,' Aisha replied. 'With us, they didn't teach in front of us, *face-to-face*. There were many girls and they were all seated in a large *hall*. Above the *hall* at the front, a room was constructed in which there was a screen' [and she gestured that it was too high to look over] and our Sir, the *muallim* used sit behind the screen and speak from there. Whatever he had to teach us, he taught from there. We could hear his voice, but his face couldn't be seen. His way upstairs was also from another direction. He didn't come into the *hall* in order to go up.' So how could the teachers check if the pupils were forming their letters correctly? 'Imagine that he had taught one lesson, and after that there would be a *recess*,' Aisha explained. 'The girls would sit in the break putting marks on their work and then would ask him afterwards. They'd tell him they didn't understand this lesson and ask him to explain it to them once more. Then he'd explain it a second time. Many times, he'd teach for 30 minutes in the 40 minutes. Then he'd say, "There are 10 minutes and you people are to read once through the lesson I've explained to you, and you should ask me about whatever you don't understand." In that way our difficulties were solved.'

But what if girls were tempted to misbehave? Were they ever punished? Aisha smiled and nodded. 'First of all, our *muallim* gave us strict instructions.' She straightened her back and adopted a stern voice and facial expression. 'He told us he was very strict and that all the girls must pay attention to their studies when he was teaching. He said that if any girl's attention wandered hither and thither, towards laughing-playing [Aisha tapped a rhythm on her bench to demonstrate], that would be against his dignity. And when we were in the *hall* studying and the *muallim saheb* was teaching, there were two *checking-masters*—they were *ladies*—wandering around the *hall*. If any girl seemed to be distracted hither and thither or was laughing and joking when Sir was teaching, the *checking-masters* used to tell the *muallim saheb*. And he'd tell them what punishment to give. These women would give the punishment, never the *muallim saheb*. They obeyed the orders of the *muallim saheb*.'

What caused a girl to be punished, then? 'First of all, not memorizing your lesson,' Aisha told us. 'And if any girl's clothes were found to be dirty, there was punishment. If any girl's bed wasn't properly arranged or it was unmethodical, then there'd be punishment. If the covers and pillow cases were dirty, there'd be punishment.' What kinds of punishments were given? 'There was both harshness and loving remonstration. Sometimes there was beating with a cane, sometimes scolding. They gave punishments according to the wrongdoing. If it was a big wrong, then the punishment was big, for a small mistake it was small. If any girl hadn't memorized her lesson, then they hit her on the hand with wood. They'd give one 50, another 35, even up to 200 hits on the hand.' And anything else? Aisha smiled broadly. 'We used to be made to do knee-bends and ear-holding. The knee-bends were also according to the studying. She who didn't study, who didn't memorize her lesson on time, would be punished accordingly.'

Aisha paused to reflect for a moment. 'Very often,' she continued, 'girls used to hide dirty clothes in their *cupboards* to wash when they had the opportunity. But if any girl forgot and hadn't washed them, and the *checking-master* saw, then there'd be punishment! And if any girl had made anything dirty in the *hostel* or wasn't keeping herself properly clean and neat, then she'd be taken out to the *passage* [outside the bedrooms] at night. That *passage* was very big and there was also complete darkness there, so they used to take the girls there to frighten them. Because of fear, a girl would say, "We won't do this wrong thing again." And then the *checking-masters* would take her back inside. Out of fear, they used to ask for forgiveness, the girls did, and would promise not to do it again!'

And was Aisha ever punished? She grinned and said that she had been punished once: 'The teacher became angry, so I had to be beaten. I was punished only on account of studying. I was beaten during my first year there, after that nothing. And that was for not memorizing my lesson. I had to do knee-bends five times—and then my legs swelled and I became sick. But it was good that the teacher put me right at the very beginning. I'd obtained a lesson for the future! And then my studies became easier. I began to study daily. I used to carry on memorizing up to 1.30 or 2.00 in the night.'

Then came another interruption—some of the younger girls from an adjacent classroom began peering through the window. Aisha told them to go away and she waved her cane at them, laughing as she did so. 'You're looking at this, *na*, the cane? Off you go!' And they ran off tittering. Did she use the cane to punish her own pupils? 'The wood has come into my hands for the first time,' she replied. 'So far, I haven't beaten anyone. But I don't know about the future!'

✳ ✳ ✳

It was clear, though, that Aisha had not found the Madrasah Islahul Banat unduly harsh. On the contrary, she clearly appreciated how the *teacher-sir* looked after the girls just like a *mother-father*. It was hard for parents to send their daughters away, she said, but they did it for the sake of education—and of course all the girls remembered their homes. 'But we had gone there to study. If you are to study, you have to tolerate a great deal. If you don't endure it, then the education will stop. My younger sister couldn't endure it, so her studies stopped. The two of us went [to Madrasah Islahul Banat], but my sister remembered our home greatly. She couldn't bear it. So she went home and her studies stopped—and she was married. If you aren't studying, then your marriage takes place. Your family thinks that you are sitting with nothing to do, so it's better to get you married! I escaped because I was studying, but my sister has been married.' Moreover, the girls were affectionate to one another: 'The girls came from such distant places, and we all lived together. We used to live with great love and affection, all praises to Allah. Everyone was very good. And one thing remained in everyone's consciousness: that we shall all be going away [from the *madrasah*] and maybe we would never meet again in this life. That was why we used to live with a lot of love. Everyone had a passion for education. Everyone wanted to obtain education.' Aisha had found the boarding *madrasah* a positive environment, where she had made friends from around the world and developed a taste for studying Islamic subjects, rather than Hindi, English, civics and history, which had appealed before she left Kashmir.

And Aisha's hopes for the future, did she want to study some more, or continue to teach? 'I have the desire to do so, if Allah wills,' Aisha said. 'May Allah-tala command the acceptance of my prayer.... In future, whatever happens will be whatever is in my destiny. And what does destiny tell you [in advance]? You only learn about it at the time!... The people in Gujarat asked me to remain there to teach, but Abbu wanted me to teach here because it's close and I would be able to live in our house in Qaziwala. That's why I began teaching here.... I've told my father that I must study some more. He said I have two more years of freedom and I can study as much as I wish, Arabic, Urdu, English, whatever I wish.' Was her father planning for her to get a good job, then? 'My father hasn't refused to let me study. He says I should study as much as I wish—there is no hindrance. But he has clearly refused to let me get service. He says that women should remain in the house but they should be educated so that they can look after the house properly. I told him that I wanted to go to Gujarat to learn how to teach, but he said he has an abhorrence of women's earnings.... He told me that if I want to teach, I should do it here [in Begawala]. What's the need to go to Gujarat? My wish to teach can be fulfilled here. Children's appropriate desires should be fulfilled—that's why I am teaching.' And once she was married? Aisha grinned. 'As long as I'm here there is no problem. But I can't predict what will happen in my in-laws' house. For it will all be under their control.'

For now, though, she would teach in the Begawala *madrasah*. Over half the *madrasah*'s 1,100 pupils were girls, but—the Principal had lamented—most would probably have left before their teens. He wanted more adolescent girls to attend, but his makeshift arrangements—a male teacher teaching on the veranda just outside the senior female teacher's classroom—were not meeting with much favor from village parents. None of the *madrasah*'s women teachers could teach advanced Islamic studies and the Principal bemoaned the difficulties of finding women suitably qualified for the task. Eventually, he had succeeded in appointing Aisha in early 2002 to teach the older girls Arabic and Farsi.

But in the villages of western Uttar Pradesh, it is controversial for a young unmarried woman such as Aisha to be employed—albeit within a sheltered *madrasah* environment. So were people gossiping about her teaching? 'People's minds are different,' Aisha said, as she launched into a spirited defence of teaching. 'People will say whatever is in their mind. You can't stop anyone's tongue. If some people say bad things, then it will "touch" your mind. You'll repeatedly feel this: why did someone talk like that? ... My desire is to study and to teach. And this is not any bad work. If anyone criticises this, just let them carry on speaking! If we think we're correct, then we shouldn't be worried about anyone else. Many women remain inside the house and nevertheless do some mixed up work—and even so people will call them good. But if a woman is compelled to go outside because of the financial state of her house, then people make up all kinds of things about her. For a woman whose husband has died and whose children are all small, it's her responsibility to make her children capable of standing on their own legs. If she leaves her job at other people's say-so, then what will she feed her children? What, will those people come and lend a hand? Will they come to give help? This is also lawful in Islam, that if a woman does not have a husband and there are small-small children, then it's her right to earn money by some permitted method and rear her children.'

'In any case,' Aisha continued, 'it's also written in the Quran Sharif, these are the words of the holy Quran: *'Talimul Quran ta alam, Alamul Quran ta alam* [teach the education of the Quran, teach the sciences of the Quran]. This means,' Aisha explained, 'that whoever has read the Quran Sharif should certainly teach it to others. You also obtain religious reward from teaching. You receive the rewards of virtue according to the number of times you have recited and taught the Quran Sharif. At the very beginning of our holy book, the letters *alif-lam-mim* have been written in this fashion' [and she wrote in the air with her fingers]. 'No one knows what this means, apart from God. They are the separate letter texts [*harfe-muqatta at*]. If you recite each of them once, you get ten times the rewards of virtue, ten times the religious merit. If you say *alif* once, you will get the same reward as if you had said it ten times. And it is like this also for *lam* and *mim*. But some people are remiss. They don't know the correct way to obtain the rewards.' Then Aisha provided an elaborate virtuoso performance to demonstrate the importance of reciting these letters correctly. First she chanted '*alif-lam-mim—alif-lam-mim—alif-lam-mim*' rapidly. 'They speak like that, very fast. In place of *mîîîim they say mim*, which is wrong. It's written in the Quran Sharif that they should be said slowly and with appreciation. Like this: *aliffff-laaaam-mîîîim*. That's the way it should be spoken. We can obtain reward without any hard work, without doing anything. Whenever we read the Quran Sharif, we utter these separate letter texts. And when we teach, we ourselves also recite. In that way, we obtain the rewards of virtue many times. We teach others as we recite. That's why it's necessary to learn goodness and to teach goodness. Whoever has read the Quran Sharif themselves should teach others to read it too.'

Is giving this kind of moral instruction more the responsibility of parents or of teachers, though? 'It's the parents' responsibility to teach their children good things, of course,' Aisha explained, 'But why do children leave their house? They go out in order to become cultured, to become courteous. People get education in order to obtain education in manners and discernment. If we ever do anything wrong, my Abbu says just one thing: "You've made all this reading-writing useless!" He only ridicules us about our education. A child goes to school to learn refinement and culture. Children are so quick-witted that they learn by themselves by watching. They see who's talking in what way, how our teachers present themselves and how they talk. Seeing this, children learn. They spend the entire day in school. They spend most of their time with their teachers, first in school, then in tuition. That's why it's also the teacher's responsibility to spend some time in school teaching good things, teaching discernment-manners. This matter is also in Islam.'

✳ ✳ ✳

As our conversation was drawing to a close, Aisha's brother came to collect her. She spent several minutes adjusting her *burqa* and veil—first with her eyes visible, and then, once she had walked along the upstairs veranda, covering her eyes with a veil in order to descend the stairs, traverse the courtyard and walk home to Qaziwala. That was the last time we saw her. By early 2003, Aisha no longer taught in the *madrasah* and she had returned to Kashmir—yet again the Principal's hopes for extending the *madrasah*'s facilities for adolescent girls were stymied.

We met Aisha's brother the following spring and he explained that Aisha had found the hot weather and monsoon intolerable in the plains. Her health had suffered and he had taken her back to Kashmir, where she was now teaching in another *madrasah*. But they were now planning to get her married in the Bijnor area, despite the climate, because she would have to make too many adjustments if she were married into a Kashmiri family.

Then, as an afterthought, he asked how Patricia knew Aisha. Were we the people who had once phoned his home asking to meet her and whom she had called to the *madrasah* to talk to her? He was puzzled. What would we have learnt from her? Aisha, he claimed, does not talk much. Hardly able to keep a straight face, Patricia contradicted him. 'You were talking about education,' he commented in response. 'That would be why she had said more. But at home she says very little.' Perhaps she was muted at home—but she had come into her own in the cloisters of the women's area in the *madrasah*, where she had talked with an enchanting energy, laughing, joking, and underscoring her points with witty and telling examples, and responding carefully and in detail to our questions. Her educational attainments—mainly but not exclusively in Islamic matters—marked her off from other young women from Qaziwala, as well as from her female colleagues in the Begawala *madrasah*. Compared with her female colleagues and pupils, she was much traveled—and she had an international network of friends, acquired through her unusual (but strictly monitored) life in a boarding *madrasah* far from home. Yet, her comings and goings between home and *madrasah* were chaperoned by her brothers and, even inside her classroom, she maintained far more stringent bodily concealment than village women did at home. Her father's willingness to brave other people's gossip had given her the space to indulge her passion for learning—but without his support this avenue would have been closed to her. And soon she would be married according to her relatives' inclinations into a family who might—or might not—permit her to continue studying and teaching.

7

Karate, Computers and the Quran Sharif: Zamir[1]

CRAIG JEFFREY, PATRICIA JEFFERY AND ROGER JEFFERY

'**K**arate, karate, KARATE!' Zamir made a chopping action and laughed while wrapping his hands round my neck. I was two years older than Zamir and two inches taller, but I didn't fancy a fight.[2] We were walking along one of the main roads leading out of Bijnor, a district town about 100 kilometres northwest of Delhi, towards the parade ground, where Zamir's karate lessons took place. He seemed in a particularly jubilant mood. 'You want to know how good I am at Karate?' He paused for effect. 'I can break a pile of stone slabs which have been doused in petrol and set alight!'

Zamir, 25 in 2001, was about 5 feet 10 inches, lean and fit. He had recently begun working out at 'Heavenly Gym', just a little further along the road into Bijnor. A friend of Zamir's had joked a few days earlier that if Zamir keeps going to lift weights he will end up looking like the man on the Heavenly

[1] Zamir is a pseudonym. This chapter is based on wider research examining how secondary schooling is changing patterns and processes of social reproduction in rural north India. We are grateful to the Economic and Social Research Council (grant number R000238495), Ford Foundation and Royal Geographical Society for funding aspects of this research, and to the Institute of Economic Growth, New Delhi, for our attachment there in 2000–2002. None bears any responsibility for what we have written here. We are also grateful to our research assistants, Swaleha Begum, Shaila Rais, Chhaya Sharma and Manjula Sharma, and to the people of Nangal and Qaziwala. We also draw on research conducted by Roger and Patricia Jeffery in 1990–91 funded by the UK's Overseas Development Administration.
[2] 'I' in this portrait refers to Craig Jeffery, the first author.

Gym sign: a boldly painted pink body-builder in red trunks with thick knots of muscle bulging in every direction. On the parade ground, Zamir took off his white prayer cap, stretched out his legs and sank his toes into the dirt. He pulled his Green Belt out of his bag and tied it round his white *kurta pyjama.* 'I'm ready to fight.'

Zamir's vigour marked him out from many of the young men we met during the course of our research into education and social change in western Uttar Pradesh (UP). His passion for karate was symptomatic of his restless energy, and signaled his disciplined approach to life, careful attention to bodily comportment, and enthusiasm for new opportunities entering Bijnor district from outside the region. Zamir was the eldest son of a rural family of middle peasant farmers living in Qaziwala, a village about 5 kilometers from Bijnor. He was unmarried and had four younger brothers, one younger sister, one older sister and two older half-sisters. Zamir's 'typical day' offers a window on his world. Up at 5 a.m., he started the day with an 8-kilometer run. Zamir had to return to milk the family's buffaloes because his mother was incapable of doing so after having had her thumb amputated following a scorpion bite. Between 7 a.m. and 10 a.m., he worked on the family's 1.7 hectares of agricultural land, sown to a rotation of sugarcane and wheat, both of which the family sold locally. His father suffered from a long-term illness and it had fallen to Zamir, as the eldest son, to take on the farming responsibilities. Zamir prepared, sowed, irrigated and fertilised the land, collected buffalo dung, drove and maintained the tractor, supervised laborers brought in for the harvest, checked on marketing arrangements and kept accounts. When we arrived for interviews in Qaziwala village, we often saw Zamir driving his tractor along the main village street: 'I'll teach you to drive this thing one day. It's good fun (*maza ata hai*)!' At 10 a.m. Zamir cycled to Bijnor for a computer class. At noon he cycled back to the village for lunch and to continue with farming work. At 3 p.m. he returned to Bijnor for karate practice followed by either an English or Advanced Accountancy tutorial. He then cycled back to Qaziwala again at 5.30 p.m. Zamir said that the rest of his day was taken up with studying for a Bachelor of Commerce degree that he was taking at the Wardhman Government Degree College in Bijnor. I ran through his 'typical day' with Zamir to check that I had the schedule right: could he *really* cycle back and forth between Bijnor twice? Does he *really* run 8 kilometers every morning? Zamir grinned when I ran through the list: 'you have forgotten one thing— I never forget to pray five times a day.'

On the same walk to karate practice, Zamir had confided that computers were his other passion in life and that he wanted to develop his knowledge of computer technology. Zamir and his parents spoke in glowing terms of the value of education. Like other Muslims in Qaziwala, they made a distinction between religious education (*dini talim*) and worldly education (*duniya ki parhai*). Religious education was available in local *madrasahs* (Islamic educational institutions) and focused on instruction in Urdu, the Quran Sharif and aspects of Islamic good practice.[3] Worldly education was available within 'mainstream' schools (schools outside the *madrasah* system) and a small number of *madrasahs*, and consisted of instruction in a range of subjects.

Zamir and his parents said that religious education and worldly education were both necessary to lead full and successful lives. Zamir's mother said that she had told her children 'study Hindi or study Urdu, but make sure you study! There is nothing without education!' Like other Muslims in Qaziwala, Zamir and his parents made a distinction between the purposes of Hindi and Urdu education. The family believed that Hindi education was important since road signs, bus timetables, doctors' prescriptions and the paper slips from the local Sugarcane Society were all in Hindi. Zamir and his parents stressed that a person unable to read Hindi was often helpless in public situations, dependent on others and vulnerable to deception. Zamir said that it was essential that his future wife should be Hindi-literate so that she could read the letters that he sent home when away from the village. Zamir even claimed on one occasion that people are 'useless' without a Hindi education. Zamir's parents, who were both unable to read or write Hindi, were similarly strident in their statements about the disadvantages of Hindi illiteracy. Zamir's father said that he felt embarrassed being unable to read, 'I don't feel right'.

Zamir and his parents also perceived Hindi education to offer a route to secure salaried employment outside Qaziwala, either in government work or private service. A class X pass was a minimum prerequisite for obtaining government employment, and many Qaziwala parents believed that further qualifications would improve their children's chances of getting a salaried job. Zamir and his parents stressed the value of government employment in particular. Government salaried work was associated in the village with a

---

[3] Y. Sikand, 2005, *Bastions of the Believers:* Madrasas *and Islamic Education in India*, New Delhi, Penguin.

secure income, prestige and a host of other benefits, such as an 'over-income' made up of bribes taken from the public, subsidised access to government welfare facilities, and a pension. For Zamir and his parents, Hindi education partly defined local ideas of development (*taraqqi*).

Whilst they perceived Hindi education to be a useful basis for seeking salaried work, Zamir and his parents viewed Urdu education as a source of knowledge about morality, good manners and religious good practice. They said that religious learning provides detailed information on how a person should pray, fast and celebrate Islamic festivals. The family imagined those educated within *madrasah*s to possess discretion, refinement and civilization. They also perceived Urdu education to open up possibilities to train to become an Islamic priest (*maulvi*) or undertake related religious work. Zamir and his parents believed that religious learning, in combination with Hindi education, transforms a person's speech, manners and comportment. They said that educated people speak politely in rounded and correctly phrased Hindi or Urdu, while illiterates converse in rude, loud and aggressive sentences. The educated dress better than the uneducated, have better standards of personal hygiene, and move around with greater poise and confidence than do illiterates. Reflecting on the connection between education and comportment, Zamir's mother asserted that, 'through studying you attain the status of a human being'. This implied that without education a person was like an animal, or savage, and some people made such assertions quite explicitly.

The schooling of Zamir's younger siblings reflected the family's enthusiasm for religious education. Zamir's younger brother, Afroz, had attended Jhandapur *madrasah* just outside Bijnor to learn Urdu and the Quran Sharif. The Jhandapur *madrasah* was opened in 1989 with remittance money from the Arab Middle East. In 2002, it had roughly 20 teachers and 400 students. Pupils at Jhandapur could also study Hindi, English and other 'worldly' subjects at a primary and lower secondary school established on the same site. Afroz left Jhandapur to study at Begawala *madrasah*,[4] which lies just outside Qaziwala on the road to Bijnor. The Begawala *madrasah* did not charge fees and it offered classes in Urdu, Islamic doctrines and the Quran Sharif. Rich local Muslims managed the *madrasah* and contributed to the running costs. *Madrasah* staff sought voluntary subscriptions in major Indian cities as a means of raising additional funds. The teachers at

---

[4] This is the *madrasah* in which Aisha taught, see Chapter 6.

Begawala also had personal links with the *Dar-ul-Ulum* seminary at Deoband, some 60 kilometers away to the west of the Ganges. After a few years at Begawala, Afroz moved to a boarding *madrasah* in Bihari Colony, Delhi, with his younger brother. Their father said that they did not have to pay fees for the *madrasah* or anything for their food and diet, but that parents paid for medicines and clothing. He said that the children take Rs 500 or Rs 1,000 back with them to Delhi when they return from holidays. In 2001, Zamir was assisting Afroz in preparing for the examinations for the *Daru-l-Ulum* seminary at Deoband. Zamir explained that out of about 200 candidates, the top 100 would pass and gain admission and the top 50 would receive scholarships. He said that the examination would contain questions on Urdu, Arabic and Farsi (Persian).

Zamir had also helped his younger sister, Rashida, to obtain a place at a girls' boarding *madrasah* in the neighboring district of Moradabad. Zamir said that his mother's brother knew the principal of the *madrasah* and had recommended the institution. Zamir went to the college to arrange admission and pay the Rs 1,500 entrance charge. Rashida had to take a test that examined students' knowledge of Urdu, Hindi and English. Rashida had been educated at Begawala *madrasah* but had also studied Hindi up to class VIII. The Moradabad *madrasah* taught Hindi, Urdu, Farsi, Arabic and English. Rashida was learning Urdu and Hindi at the institution alongside a six-year course that would qualify her to teach small children. The *madrasah* was run privately and charged fees of Rs 500 a month, which included food. Both Zamir and his mother spoke of the advantages of the girls' boarding *madrasah* over a Bijnor secondary school. Zamir's mother asked what people would say if they saw her daughter 'coming and going to Bijnor every day on the road'. Zamir spoke of the excellent discipline at the *madrasah*, and described how the institution 'guarded her—so the family don't have to worry'. He explained that all the teachers at the Moradabad *madrasah* were Muslim women and that there was a hostel at the *madrasah* where girls' activities were strictly supervised. At the time of admission, *madrasah* staff insisted that Zamir and his maternal uncle write down their names, which were kept at the *madrasah* alongside their photographs. Zamir said that no other man could visit his sister at the hostel and that staff always checked his appearance against the photo. He commented enthusiastically on the strictness of the teachers and their careful attention to ensuring that girls did not wander outside the *madrasah* gates. 'Boys are not allowed anywhere near the school!'

Zamir's depictions of *madrasahs* contrasted markedly with images of *madrasah* education circulating in South Asia in 2000 and 2001. Even before the attacks on America on 11 September 2001, sections of the Indian government and media were depicting *madrasahs* as terrorist training grounds that instilled fundamentalism and intolerance. After 9/11 these allegations became more strident. With renewed force, parts of the Indian and foreign media accused *madrasahs* of hiding stashes of arms, sponsoring cross-border terrorism, receiving foreign funding for disreputable purposes and propagating militant Islam. Zamir appeared unconcerned by these accusations and rumors. Without directly alluding to the stories circulating in the media, he depicted *madrasahs* as spaces of order, patient learning and civility.

Zamir's own educational career, though, reflected his primary interest in Hindi education as a route to social mobility. Zamir had a passion for mathematics. He loved logical problems, word games and number puzzles. Notebook and pencil in his top pocket, his eyes would light up when presented with a conundrum or brainteaser. Aware of this enthusiasm, Zamir's parents enrolled him at the Qaziwala Government Primary School at the same time as encouraging him to attend the Begawala *madrasah*. The Qaziwala Government Primary School, however, was symptomatic of the UP government's failure to provide educational facilities.[5] The school was located in a small two-roomed building that contained a blackboard and numerous broken chairs and tables. Many parents in Qaziwala said that teachers were often absent from class or arrived tired, drunk or unwilling to teach. Teachers often sat on the veranda of the school knitting or drinking tea. Several parents also said that the teachers discriminated against Muslims. Zamir told us that he was disappointed with the school and wanted to build a good school for Muslim children in Qaziwala.

While studying in Begawala *madrasah*, Zamir learnt to read and write Urdu and recite the Quran from memory (*Hafyz Quran*). In spite of this success, however, he saw his future in worldly education. At the age of 12 or

---

[5] See Roger Jeffery, Patricia Jeffery and Craig Jeffrey, 2005, 'Social Inequalities and the Privatisation of Secondary Schooling in North India', in Radhika Chopra and Patricia Jeffery (eds), *Educational Regimes in Contemporary India*, New Delhi: Sage Publications, pp. 41–61; Patricia Jeffery, Roger Jeffery and Craig Jeffrey, 2007, 'Investing in the Future: Education in the Social and Cultural Reproduction of Muslims in UP', in Mushirul Hasan (ed.), *Living with Secularism: The Destiny of India's Muslims*, New Delhi: Manohar, pp. 63–89; and R. Sachar, 2006, *Social, Economic and Educational Status of the Muslim Community in India*, New Delhi, Cabinet Secretariat, Government of India.

13, Zamir left the government primary school and Begawala *madrasah* to enter secondary school at Bijnor Inter College (BIC). BIC was a privately managed senior secondary school on the outskirts of the town offering classes from VI to XII. It catered mainly for the poor, many of whom were Muslims. Zamir remembered his secondary schooling as a struggle to pass examinations and move successfully from one class to the next. He also spoke of how some teachers often failed to teach properly in class. He said that teachers at BIC occasionally threatened to fail students in examinations if they did not arrange to take expensive private tuition with them outside classes. Zamir also remembered teachers who inspired their pupils and provided role models, however. He recalled that one teacher, Nabil, gave poor children free tuitions. Zamir said that he agreed with Nabil's philosophy that education should be a right rather than a privilege: 'I think that education should be the same for everyone.'

Zamir learnt from an early age that his chances of obtaining a good education and going on to capture a secure salaried job might depend on his ability to bribe those in positions of authority. Corruption in the marking of school examinations is a marked feature of the Bijnor educational scene, at least up to class IX. Zamir said that children in classes VI, VII and VIII in BIC were able to improve their marks in the yearly examinations through developing a good relationship with teachers or through giving them a bribe (*rishwat, ghus*). Zamir said that many pupils who narrowly failed examinations could persuade the teacher to 'nudge up their marks' by offering a small amount of cash. Zamir contrasted this corruption within mainstream schooling with procedures organized by *madrasahs*. He said that the *Dar-ul-Ulum* examinations his younger brother would take were completely 'straight' (*sidha*) and did not involve considerations of personal influence.

After passing his class X (High School) examinations from BIC, Zamir decided to move to the Government Inter College (GIC) in Bijnor. Unlike most government schools in Bijnor district, GIC had a reputation for providing a relatively high standard of teaching. In addition, Zamir had already decided by class X that he wanted to carry on after Senior High School to do a degree in Commerce. He was concerned that BIC did not offer a Mathematics course in classes XI and XII and that this would prevent him entering the Commerce stream. Zamir got the 50 percent marks in his class X examinations which he needed to enter GIC.

Zamir went on to get 72 percent in his class XII examinations in GIC, well clear of the 64 percent he needed to enroll in a Bachelor of Commerce degree at Wardhman Degree College. Zamir enrolled to study 'old' rather than 'new' commerce at Wardhman. Old commerce provided a broader grounding in commerce, accountancy and related topics than new commerce. People also connected old commerce with opportunities to obtain government employment. Zamir remembered how a recent advertisement for public-sector positions within the postal service specified that candidates should have studied old commerce. Zamir explained that students taking new commerce were just doing their degrees 'to pass the time'.

A Qaziwala villager described Wardhman Degree College to us as a place 'where teachers don't teach and students don't learn'. While studying at Wardhman, Zamir had become painfully aware of the failure of the UP State to provide broad-based higher education of a reasonable quality. Zamir told us that when he arrived for classes at Wardhman, the lecturer told the students to arrange private tuitions if they wanted to learn anything. Zamir said that he was keen to avoid taking tuitions for his degree but that circumstances had compelled him to do so. 'If you didn't, you wouldn't learn anything.' Zamir took tuitions in Advanced Accounting and English. He said that the Advanced Accounting was for his career and the English was for his own knowledge. Zamir was enthusiastic about learning English, though he was unable to speak it. The two tutorials cost Rs 350 each a month, but showing typical initiative, Zamir had managed to negotiate with the Advanced Accounting tutor to pay only Rs 300. Zamir said that tuitions had become so popular that many of his peers hardly bothered to go to Wardhman College itself, or, if they went, it was just to chat, meet friends or pass time.

Zamir's energy contrasted markedly with the attitude of some of his peers, and he criticised young men who spent their lives 'wandering about' or 'just passing time'.[6] The failure of many students in and around Qaziwala to obtain secondary school qualifications had contributed to the emergence of moral narratives focussed around images of aimless, errant, irresponsible and rebellious young men. In line with these narratives, Zamir contrasted the lax attitude of many students in local schools or colleges to the strictness of boarding in a *madrasah*, where he said students followed a rigorous programme of activity.

---

[6] See Craig Jeffrey, Patricia Jeffery and Roger Jeffery, 2008, *Degrees without Freedom? Education, Masculinities and Unemployment in North India,* Stanford: Stanford University Press.

By the end of his secondary school career, Zamir was already thinking about how he might build on his enthusiasm for mathematics by developing computer competency. During the 1990s, five computer institutes had sprung up in Bijnor town each offering to provide students with a suite of skills relevant to their future employment. Zamir and two school friends each decided to enroll in a different computing institute for a short trial. After three days, they met to compare their experiences. They decided that a small newly-opened institute on the outskirts of Bijnor would provide the best education, and Zamir paid Rs 1,200 to enrol in a three-year computer course there. Students at the computer institute were organized into batches of eight and worked two to a computer during the one-hour daily class. They spent one day doing written work and the next day doing practical exercises on the computers. Zamir said that standards of supervision were high and that outside computing tuition was unnecessary. He had already learnt DOS and Microsoft Windows. Zamir saw his present course as a stepping-stone to further computer knowledge: he wanted to proceed to a course with the Software Technology Group (STG) which had opened a training center in Bijnor. Zamir was hopeful that he could use agricultural profits to finance an STG course, which would cost a total of Rs 53,000. Zamir spoke enthusiastically of the alleged 'good links' between the Bijnor STG group and institutions in the USA. Zamir noted confidently, 'computing is the future'.

Zamir linked computing to opportunities to obtain secure salaried work (*pakki naukri*), preferably within the government. The liberalization of the Indian economy had resulted in a decline in the availability of government jobs at a time when there was increasing competition for posts. Many young men arrived at written examinations for jobs to find that several thousand candidates were applying for fewer than 10 positions. In addition, applications for a government job could take two years to be processed and involved considerable travel, repeated tests and prolonged attempts to chivvy relatives, friends and acquaintances into providing financial, moral or practical support.

Like many other educated young men in Bijnor district, Zamir had already tried unsuccessfully to obtain government work. During a physical test for the army, the doctor told Zamir that his heart rate was too fast. His father said that Zamir should have given the doctor a bribe, and Zamir spoke of endemic corruption (*bhrashtachar*) within the cut-throat competition for government posts. Like other young Muslim men in Qaziwala, Zamir stated that something like a 'price list' existed for different government jobs. At the bottom of the scale, he claimed that people paid about Rs 40,000 or 50,000 to become a police officer, while at the top of the price list, people might spend Rs 400,000 to obtain the post of District Magistrate. Zamir said that it was occasionally possible to get a salaried job without paying a bribe, for example if you had very good social contacts (*jan pehchan*). He explained that he could not just walk into an office and give an official a bribe, but would have to work through a broker (*dalal*), who would accompany him to Bijnor, assist him in negotiations with recruitment officials and might also provide a recommendation (*sifarish*). According to Zamir: 'Three things are necessary to get a salaried job: of most importance is money, then social contacts, then knowledge. Often those who have very good education don't get salaried jobs because they don't give bribes. This is wrong; those who are very well educated should get salaried work.' Yet, unlike some rural Muslims, who reported facing discrimination on the grounds of their religion during their attempts to obtain government work, Zamir did not comment on communalism within processes of recruitment.

Zamir had begun to plan how to escape the corruption of government employment markets. He said that there was much less bribery for jobs requiring computer skills within the government than for other posts. He maintained that people without computing skills who secured a government position through bribery found it impossible to do their job. Zamir said that people in the office would ask the new appointee, 'okay, you've got the job, but what can you do on the computer?' Zamir therefore saw computing as a means of obtaining government employment without having to pay a bribe. Zamir was ambivalent about corruption, however. Although often critical of bribery in processes of recruitment to government work, he said that he would pay a bribe if it ensured his entry into a government post. Zamir claimed that for a class II or class III government job,[7] he might have to pay Rs 40,000 or 50,000, but for a good salaried post he was ready to spend Rs 100,000. Zamir also said that if he got a government job that allowed him to collect bribe money, he would do so. 'Why not? When you see bribes being taken for all sorts of work, I think that I should also take these bribes.' Zamir was pragmatic about his chances of getting salaried work, though. 'If we don't get a salaried job we just think that it is a matter of fate (*nasib*), fate (*taqdir*) [repeated loudly]! If, after so much study and so

---

[7] Government jobs are organized into four classes (I to IV) based on the nature of an office holder's responsibilities. Class I posts are the most senior.

much trying, we still fail to get salaried work, we become sad and angry. When we sit together, we become frustrated about this sometimes; but this frustration only lasts 10 or 15 days.'

Another man interjected at this point, 'Then their father will tell them to stop being fools, and get up and do some work.' Zamir repeated that after a while they realize that it is not their fate to get salaried employment and they should do some other work. Zamir was already preparing for this eventuality by thinking about business opportunities outside the village. He regularly went to Delhi to contact friends who worked as tailors or embroiderers in the capital, partly to keep abreast of employment opportunities outside Bijnor district. He pointed out that, 'Computers are a very useful skill for business.' Zamir sometimes appeared unsure about whether the quest for government work was worthwhile, and he occasionally appeared to envy his brother, Afroz. Zamir contrasted the 'straight' system through which Afroz would seek out positions as a *maulvi* with the complexities and duplicities of corruption within government employment markets. Zamir said that there was no question of bribery or social influence in people's attempts to become *maulvi*s 'it all just happens in a fair way'. Zamir also noted that to work as a *maulvi* provides religious as well as financial rewards.

In wearing explicitly Islamic clothes, Afroz risked antagonizing state officials, who were mostly upper-caste Hindus. Many Muslims who had worked in urban areas of western UP or Delhi complained about intimidation from the mainly Hindu police force. In embracing an Islamic identity, Afroz bore the risk of police intimidation, including threats, unlawful arrest or even attack and murder. In the context of wider rumors about people organizing protests against the bombing in Afghanistan, Zamir described how the Superintendent of Police in Bijnor had told people to put their address in their top pocket if they were thinking of taking out a demonstration, 'So we know where to send the body'. When I asked Zamir why he was learning karate, he told me that people were increasingly worried about being attacked on the streets and that karate provided a form of self defence. It was not clear whether Zamir was referring to threats to people in general or Muslims in particular. On another occasion, however, Zamir said that he and other Muslims did not live in daily fear of attack in Bijnor, and he stressed that karate was also a means of keeping fit, building concentration and making friends with people from various backgrounds.

The aftermath of the attacks on America on 11 September 2001 further politicized the process through which young men sought employment within *madrasah*s and cultivated Islamic identities in rural Bijnor district. Rising communal tensions related to two sets of processes. On the one hand, the then Hindu nationalist Indian government used the pretext of a global Islamic terrorist threat to circulate fears of a 'Muslim danger' in UP. This appeared to strengthen the hand of the police force in Bijnor district. On 15 October 2001, the Superintendent of Police in Bijnor instigated police shootings in which three young Muslim men died, one of whom was from Qaziwala. On the other hand, in response to the US-led bombing of Afghanistan on 16 October 2001, the *Dar-ul-Ulum* seminary issued a *fatwa* advising Muslims to avoid all products manufactured by American or British companies. One of Zamir's friends made it clear that, 'We think both Osama and George Bush are in the wrong. Osama should not have attacked America and George Bush should not have attacked Afghanistan.' But Zamir appeared disinterested. He was reluctant to talk about world affairs and preferred to focus on his own hobbies, education, religion and family. After an attempt to draw out his political opinions he told me: 'There are really just two things in my life...computers...[he paused and raised his hand] and KARATE!'

8

Poor, Untouchable, Muslim and Mirasi
Abdul, the Storyteller

SHAIL MAYARAM

For the storyteller of storytellers, Komal Kothari (1929–2004)

The invitation to write for this book became an opportunity to revisit the landscape of one's memory and think about the many Muslims whom I came to know and learn from. So which of these could I write about? There was Bai, a part of my childhood. She worked for us as cook and housekeeper in our old, rambling house in the Sagar cantonment, in central India. It had a clay tiled roof, so housekeeping meant the constant strategic placing of buckets to catch leaks from the heavy monsoon rain and their constant emptying. Diwali meant Bai's *gujiya*s, a melt-in-your-mouth pastry, that no one has ever been able to replicate. Over the years Bai's entire family was woven into our lives. My mother made sure that her many children got educated and employed. A daughter grew up to be a competent nurse, one son a university employee, another a reputed mechanic....For years the family would come to meet my mother whenever they visited Sagar and even came to stay with us in Jaipur.

Today as I see so many children growing up in middle-class families in virtually mono-religious neighborhoods and schools, I think also of the several friendships my parents had with Muslims. Professor Ali of the Geography Department and his wife who brought with her the culture and cuisine of Aligarh's landed gentry. Her *pan dan* containing betel nut leaves and condiments which was her invariable accompaniment remains imprinted in my memory. Another Muslim wife on campus was known for the expletives that spiced her speech, *voh kambakhta daktar*....

The tragedy of our times is that we seem to be adopting rather than interrogating the American model of ethnically homogenous neighborhoods for our cities. In our case the boundaries are religious rather than racial as inhabitants refer to predominantly Muslim localities as 'Pakistan' denying them housing and upwardly mobile livelihoods.

An involvement with social movements can, however, often undercut the boundaries of middle-class, urban lives. Indeed, the association with a highly active feminist and civil liberties movement in Jaipur brought me in touch with many Muslims. There was Nishat Hussain who lived a largely uneventful life till the growing culture of violence catapulted her out of her placid middle-class existence. She lived in a predominantly Hindu neighborhood in the crowded commercial district of Jaipur's Jauhari Bazaar within the walled city. Nishat fought both the ethnicization of the city and patriarchies among Muslims through the All India Muslim Women's Welfare Association that she established. It played an important role in conflict resolution, Muslim education and negotiation with the state on behalf of Muslims detained under the draconian Terrorist and Disruptive Activities Prevention Act (TADA). There was also Vaqqar-ul-Ahad who belonged to a particular genus of the Indian Muslim experience, that of the radical Muslim. Communist, trade union activist, lawyer and former legislator, Vaqqar Saab had an intimate knowledge of the walled city and its neighborhoods that came from his movement through the area on foot and bicycle. Following major riots in Jaipur (1989, 1990) when a Hindutva-oriented political culture influenced the state ministry and bureaucracy, civil society and sections of the judiciary, Vaqqar-ul-Ahad was one of the few persons who got Muslims to file petitions and continued to wage what was a hopeless battle within the aegis of the Tibrewal Commission set up by the Government of Rajasthan to identify responsibility for the communal riots..

Over the years as I have grown into an academic, I also feel privileged to have known closely another genus, that of the liberal Muslim: Muzaffar Alam, pre-eminent medievalist questioning historiographical shibboleths; Asghar Ali Engineer, reformist and author of numerous riot studies; Mushirul Hasan, historian and, perhaps, the most fervent Nehruvian secularist and academic exponent of Muslim nationalism that I can think of; Imtiaz

Ahmad, sociologist and pioneer of Muslim studies in India, battling for democratic choices, alliances and alternatives.

It was, however, the research on the Meo Muslims that became a profound experience of reschooling and unlearning, destabilizing my census-derived certainties and lenses. A decade and half of work on the Meos taught me about the many different ways of being Muslim. There were many Meos whom I could write about, but it is the Mirasi to the Meo who commands this portrait. And who better than Abdul of Maujpur?

Abdul. Untouchable. Muslim. From a service caste referred to as *kamin*. Illiterate. Like the rest of his Mirasi community he inhabits a world where his art is seen as passé. Yet he is part of a living tradition that derives from a millennium-old literary universe of *kavya, katha vaccana* and *gathas*. This is the oral tradition of Mewati, which draws upon Sanskrit, Persian and the many vernaculars that flourished in the medieval 'vernacular millennium' of the Indian subcontinent.

As Abdul begins singing-reciting, one notes that his voice lacks the tonal quality of several other Mirasis and Manganiyars, another caste of performing artists. But he makes up for it with his enormous repertoire. Magical universes open up in its play of lyric verse and prose. I have known Abdul since 1985. He is now toothless and hard of hearing, but as sprightly and articulate as ever. Over the years I have gone back to him, again and again, to learn about Mewati narratives. I revisited Abdul in February 2004 to share with him my new book, *Against History, Against State*—he has been an important part of its making. The Mewat countryside is plush yellow with the mustard crop in full bloom camouflaging the four years of drought the villagers of this desert state have lived through.

A tattered bedspread dries on the clothes line as I talk to the family. After decades of work they own hardly any land. They live in a Meo neighborhood of a village called Maujpur, which is near Lacchmangarh town in Alwar district. For years the household has depended on Abdul's caste occupational work and the harvests and generosity of peasant-patrons. Abdul was finally able to save enough to buy less than an acre of land. He sold it to buy the plot they live on at present as his son wanted to live closer to the road. As a Below Poverty Line (BPL) household Abdul tells me he got Rs 16,000 from the government and built a brick and mortar house. Abdul and Palto now live with their five granddaughters and four grandsons in the two small rooms they built. During construction, they ran out of money so that the walls of a room and a kitchen are only half built.

Abdul was born in Nyana near Govindgarh. He compresses communal memory in a signature verse, '*Govindgarh ka sattasi main, navasi main bhaga-bhag*' (The Revolt of Govindgarh in 1931–32, the fleeing-running in 1947).[1] These two events of the peasant revolt against the monarch and the genocide of partition frame his childhood and adolescence. He did not see people fighting or dying in the first, but recalls that '*tafsis* [surveillance] took place by the *chilgari* [literally "vulture vehicle" or aeroplane]. It was in the month of *phagun* [Indian spring or March]....We were afraid and hid in the mustard field.' Partition was particularly traumatic, 'In 1947, I hid with my book, my *ilm* [knowledge/learning], in a baniya's shop. The *dhar* [mob] came from Pahatvada [in the Bharatpur kingdom]. It took away my books hidden in the trunk. Gujars and Minas came in the *dhar*, also Chamars....'

I probe Palto's memory. She cannot recall when she was married; it was 'so long ago'. Her hands, gnarled and wrinkled, rest on the cot. She peers at me from a single exposed eye, the rest of her face veiled by a synthetic mauve *dupatta* that she wears with her orange Meoni suit and sparse silver jewelry. Her natal home was in Ladla, in Kaman, in a village of the Nai Meos that was under the rule of the Bharatpur Maharaja. Caste and *gotra* (exogamous patrilineal clans) determine the norms of kinship relations among both Meos and Mirasis. So while Palto belongs to the Momia *gotra*, Abdul's family is of the Dissar *gotra*.

In contrast, Abdul's memory is remarkable for its clarity. At one time, he tells me, he had such a sharp memory that he would learn verses at one go. 'During the *bhaga-bhagi* I first went to Pathrali. But [villages like] Pathrali and Toli ka bas on the border [of Rajputana] also started fleeing. They all collected in *angreji* [British India]. [The Meo leader] Chaudhary Yasin said, don't flee. But [another Meo leader] Sardar Khan said, they will make you *shudh* [literally purify], change your *mazhab* [convert you]. Come to Pakistan, he said. [There were] so many people on the Kala Pahar [the Aravalli mountains bordering the Alwar kingdom]. Then the firing took place. The military of the Alwar raja started firing. I went to Adbar in Haryana. The world was going in a *kafila* (convoy) to Pakistan. I also got ready to go. I had two older brothers, each had a daughter. They got such severe pox that we were unable to go.... *Shuddhi* took place in many villages for six months, one year. Shammi in Maujpur became *shudh*. From Adbar I went to Nuh where I lived for two-three years.'

[1] S. Mayaram, 1997, *Resisting Regimes: Myth, Memory and the Shaping of a Muslim Identity*, New Delhi: Oxford University Press.

Palto and Abdul had been married at that time, but Palto's *gauna* [rite of departure to the marital home] had not taken place. Coincidentally her parents arrived in Haryana some six-seven months after Abdul. Given the circumstances, it was a simple ritual, no expenses entailed. Palto protests at Abdul's description, '*Byaha main to khub diyo*' [my parents spent a good amount in the wedding). 'I was the only child,' she states.

Abdul's father was a professional musician and did '*birat ka kam*' (ritual work relating to Meo marriages such as delivering invitations). Abdul's marriage was fortuitous; Palto's uncle, Bhure Khan of Rosia, became his *ustad* (teacher). It was from this popular musician of Kaman (Bharatpur) that he derives the range of his repertoire including the *Rana Sanga ki bat, Alamgir, Jaitun, Asavari* and *Pandun ki bat.*

A semblance of normalcy was restored only a few years after partition. Abdul's father and brothers settled in Maujpur. The family's small landholding of two acres had been lost to Punjabi migrants from across the border. Over a period, six daughters and a son were born to the couple. A part of Abdul's family that migrated to Pakistan settled in Bhawalpur, Lahore and Multan. They got land only in 1984. 'This was the year that I had gone to visit them,' Abdul's son tells me. 'But Pakistani Muslims such as the self-styled maliks and shaikhs look down upon us...discriminate against us' (*dekhte giri nazar se...bhed bhav karte*). 'They call us *muhajir*. There are 500 Mirasi households there. Some sing, but most of them now do "service".'

Pundlot Meos from Itarana, near Alwar, are presently the neighbors of Abdul's family. 'While there has always been *hukka-pani* [a way of denoting social interaction] between us, poor persons like Mirasis would be fed at their homes, but they would not eat at ours,' Abdul's son tells me.

'Is untouchability countered by the influence of the Tablighi Jamaat?' I ask.

While the global organization of the Tablighis is committed to equality and reformist Islam it is, nonetheless, hierarchical in its own institutional structure. In India Mirasis still continue to experience caste discrimination. I witnessed on my last visit with Abdul, the disparaging, downgrading attitude of even an educated Meo. I had taken him to visit a Meo known for his knowledge of poetry. '*Yeh to mangane-khane vali kaum hai, yeh mirasi kya jane*,' the Meo said, alluding to Mirasi dependence on the Meos as an untouchable caste of musicians.

My question occasions an insight into the sectarian divisions rife among Meos and Mirasis. 'We are *Alvarvale* and not *Dillivale*,' assert the male members of Abdul's family who have gathered during the course of our conversation. 'The *Alvarvale* are Sunni (Ahl-i Sunnat wa Jamaat), the *Dillivale* are called Wahhabi.' The Alwar school, affiliated to Deoband, based at Alwar's Daudpur Madrasah is led by Nanhemiyan from Delhi. The Delhi group follows the traditional style (*purane tariqe se kam karte*). In Rajasthan 60 per cent Meos are estimated to be Barelwis who follow a 'customary' model of Islam, but in nearby Haryana 90 per cent Meos are with the Tablighi Jamaat. 'Oh yes, they fight and make sarcastic statements about each other. Just recently there was a battle near the Mil Madrasah,' I am told.

To begin with, Abdul dismisses sectarian differences stating that both have similar concerns, *sach bolo, chori mat karo, anyaya mat karo* [tell the truth, don't steal, don't be unjust]. Then he adds, 'They [*Dillivale*] say, do not offer *fatihah* [ritual reading of the Quran] to the dead on the third day after death. *Pir-paigambar ko mat mano. Saj-baj bhi galat. Band karein. Dilli vala Mirasi se bhi chire. Shadi-byah main jayein. Ruko, gao mat. Gana bajana mat karo. Jo kuch likha hai mil jayega* [Do not follow pirs and paigambars. Playing instruments is also wrong. Stop it. The Delhiwallahs dislike the Mirasis. When they come to marriages they say, Stop, don't sing. Stop singing and playing. You will get whatever amount you were promised].'

'Have you ever participated in Tablighi Jamaat congregations,' I persist?

Abdul replies in a style characteristic of him, bringing out what is called the sweetness of spoken Mewati, '*Ab ye bat ku mat pucho. Baghora main jalsa hue. Hazratji ayo Dilli valo. Phainta maine bhi Dilli vale ke pairon main rakha. Jhut nay bolun* [Now don't ask me this. A congregation was held in the area of the Baghora Pal. Hazratji of Delhi came. I also placed my turban at his feet. I won't lie].'

Placing his turban at the feet of Hazrat In'amul Hasan al Kandhalawi (1965–95) signified Abdul's shift of sectarian affiliation. But it is obviously not a full-scale turnaround! Abdul did not give up his singing till advancing age made it difficult, and his mobility became impaired.

On my most recent visit we sat on string cots under a tree in front of their home; the cot is covered with a green and white patchwork *gudri*, a coverlet crafted by Abdul's granddaughter. Palto sports a parrot green *salwar kameez*, a shawl covers her head. Abdul wears a *kurta* and a black and white *tahmad* (lungi, now seen as appropriate Muslim men's wear replacing the older dhoti). As we talk I observe how his ruddy brown skin is broken by deep creases. He wears a beard, but also a moustache and thick frames for his fading eyesight. An occasional tractor passes on the lazy road, sometimes a cyclist with provisions. A granddaughter and grandson stand in the background. Two of his other granddaughters sit with their young children. I catch up on the joys and travails of the family. Mahmoodi, the daughter-in-law, has been possessed by a spirit and is being treated by a nearby *bhagat*, a healer of the Yadav caste. The granddaughter who is cooking *roti*s on the *chulha* (traditional earthen oven) is to be married. Abdul tells me that he cannot go out with us in the evening as he has to receive his guests, the prospective husband's family.

Ever so often Abdul interrupts our conversation with verse, this time from a narrative with an Islamic theme. '*Yeh bhi shayari, lekin hadis se shayari juri hui, hadis ka nichor hai ismai* [This is poetry, but poetry connected to the Hadith, with the essence of the Hadith],' he says. Folk Islam, certain scholars have called it, but it has its own negotiations with theology.

I ask about the Goddess of Dhaulagarh, whom I have heard him invoke in the framing verses of a Mewati narrative called *Harsana ki bat*. This is the goddess celebrated by Mirasis:

> i bhoa ki binti devi tu achcho dijai gyan
> bhai achcho dijai gyan khol hirday ka tala
> hirdai baiho an pet main karo ujala
> ye satyug ki bat sabhi akkal ka tala
> meri maf karo taksir sabha main sunai vala
> nagarkot jvala bai meri ek araj su ley
> aisi gail bata dai gyan ki sabha main vah vah dai

It is Bhola (the poet's) plea, devi, give the right knowledge.
Give the right knowledge, open the locks of the mind.
Be seated in my heart, light up my inside.
In the age of truth, all minds are closed.
Forgive the mistakes, all those who listen in the audience.
In Nagarkot[2] the flame glows brighter, listen to my request.
Show me the path to knowledge that the audience might celebrate.

---

[2] Literally means walled city, but more likely a place near Alwar which has a temple of the Dhaulagadh devi. It is suggested that this place is more important than the temples of the devi's sister at Jwala, Kailadevi, Sanchor, and Mansadevi. Revered by poets, the devi is worshipped by both Hindus and Muslims particularly in Dhaulagadh because this is a largely Muslim area.

Most people, however, would not regard Abdul as, ritually speaking, an observant Muslim. He confesses with a laugh, '*Jab mevan ki mahfil jurti to sharab bhi pi*' (I have also consumed alcohol at Meo gatherings). He refers to Palto as '*mujhse jada paband—roza-namaz main*,' implying that she is more rule-bound than him when it comes to performing the canonical Islamic *namaz* prayer and the Ramzan fast. This is possibly because the month of fasting often overlaps with the marriage season among the Meos when the Mirasi is much in demand for his combination of ritual, entertainment and cultural performance-related roles.

Abdul's income has been shrinking: the bridal party no longer makes a week-long-stay at Meo weddings and the cultural space for the oral performance tradition that depended on the community's patronage has shrunk. Islamic reformism that downgrades the visual and performing arts as unIslamic has exacerbated the effects of social and economic change. The electronic and communications revolution has brought television into homes, bringing with it new media and new entertainers. Abdul's son has given up his caste occupation and instead works for an upholstery shop in Nuh. His grandson works occasionally as a barber and since it is the Diwali season has gone to help his father. The daughter-in-law earns a mere Rs 20–40, minimum wage regulations notwithstanding, for cutting grass.

'*Vo bat nay*,' Palto tells me, suggesting how times have become more difficult. Once Rs 20 had great value. The Mirasi is still required at Meo weddings, but nowadays there are tapes and radios. Even tractors play cassettes, she says.

Abdul elaborates on how things have changed recently. 'When it is a matter of self-interest then Subedar stands for me and I for the Subedar,' he says, gesturing to an ex-army Meo sitting with us. '*Lekin ab dil saf nahin*' (people's hearts are not pure), he says. 'In the aftermath of the Babri Masjid demolition Hindus even stopped *len-den* [transactions] with us. [This was when] in the rural areas we kept up such *bhaichara* [brotherhood]—even with the Punjabis who took our lands.' The Subedar adds, 'After the Babri Masjid [demolition] political parties like the BJP, Bajrang Dal, Hindu Parishad, and Shiva Sena do not have the *bhavna* [feelings/attitude] they should have.' '[But] Meos are more *wafadar* [patriotic] than others,' he concludes.

Sometime ago Palto visited Pakistan traveling through Lyallpur and Lahore for four months. Abdul did not go as he was looking after the children. Palto's nephew has a medical shop but she compares it unfavorably with India, '*Aisa na lage jaise apna mulk*' (it is not like our country). Marriages continue to be of Meos with Meos and of Mirasis with Mirasis (along community lines), but they have begun marrying with the *phuphi's* (father's sister's) children. '*Apna Maujpur sabse accha. Vahan garib bahut*' (Our Maujpur is the best. Pakistan has many poor people), Palto comments.

I once recorded from Abdul a 'genealogical' account (akin to the form of a *jati purana*) of the Meos called the *Palon ki Bansabali* (Alwar, 29 September 1989). The category 'origin myth' flattens and reduces what such accounts are about and, indeed, such genealogies can assume many forms. One such form is the *sthala purana* that describes origins and details local terrain. Others relate to historical processes involving migration and settlement and might even refer to the dissolution and amalgamation of castes. One such account of the Shrimal merchant caste, for instance, describes their migration from the medieval city of Bhinmal in Rajasthan.

The genre of the *vanshavali* (genealogical account) is indispensable to the identity of the many castes and communities of India. In the case of the Meos it outlines their clan structure, the core of their social and political institutions. But the description of the cultural collective that locates the community in time and space points to larger connections that have to do with webs of cosmic and social time. The area of Mewat that is the land of the Meos, is adjacent to Brajbhumi, the land of the cowherd god Krishna. From Krishna, Abdul's account tells us, came the Jats and also the Meo clans, both known as Jadu kshatriyas, the warrior groups of the *vansh* of the Yadavas. From Krishna descend five Jadu clans while Arjun is the founder of four Tonwar Meo clans and the remaining two clans are descended from Rama. The Vaishnava moorings of the genealogy are explicit and the Meos' identification with Brajbhumi marked in their language and vocabulary.

Sociologists and historians have often superimposed a 'functional' reading on genealogies viewing the claim to 'kshatriya' status as a strategy oriented to aspirations of status, land and power. But in the case of the Meos it marks also a collective memory of loss of power and the erosion of autonomy by a series of state forms beginning in the early medieval period. As I have pointed out elsewhere, the Meos have a history of resistance to the state that is unparalleled anywhere in the world.[3]

Bat (from the Rajasthani *vat*) is the generic name for 'historical' narratives in the Mewati oral tradition. The term means 'tale' or 'epic' or prose narrative

[3] S. Mayaram, 2003, *Against History, Against State: Counterperspectives from the Margins*, New York and London: Columbia University Press.

and derives from the Sanskrit *varta* or account. *Vat* are authored, preserved and transmitted by bardic castes like the Charan, Bhat, Mirasi and Rao. Ziegler points out that since *vat* relates to constructions of an event they are far more historical than the *khyat* and *pirhiavali* or *vanshavali* that may be translated as panegyric and genealogy respectively.[4] In form, rhyme and meter, *vat sahitya* (literature) is not very different from written poetical composition and exposes the artificial dichotomy between oral and written, folk and classical.

The role of imagination and perspective is marked in Meo and other oral traditions. This is in contrast to the genre of written history where the narrator is screened off, hidden from view except to the discerning reader armed with weapons of deconstruction. There are also no inflated claims of authorship qua intellectual property and copyright. Indeed, this has landed the Manganiyar musicians in some trouble as their own compositions have been appropriated and copyrighted by Bollywood.

The strands of a pronounced historical consciousness have been apparent to me again and again in Abdul's narratives. He relates Mewati *bat* to the Persian category of *tawarikh* (chronicles, histories). Many Mirasis would echo his claim, '*ham mevon ki tawarikh kahte hain*' (we narrate the histories of the Meos). Abdul's treasure trove of remembered events are often an account of the state-community as also inter-community relations, a communal archive, as it were. On one occasion he told me of the battle that took place at the time of Akbar between the Meos and Minas since when, he said, they have been in a state of *bigra-bigri* (feud).

One of the earliest narratives I recorded from Abdul is called *Govindgarh* (Alwar, 1 January 1988), about the major peasant revolt of the 1930s. Abdul's version, which I have detailed in *Resisting Regimes*, is really a perspective of the Duhlot clan. A parallel but different narrative of this revolt is available to us in the story called *Dhamukar* that describes the event through the lens of the Baghora clan. The contrast between *Govindgarh* and *Dhamukar* suggests how the same event is interpreted differently by the narrative tradition. Abdul's account gives us a sense of the community's construction of 'leadership' as also of its non-leadership. That is, even though there were many leaders of the Meo movement, the narrative

---

[4] N. P. Ziegler, 1976, 'The Seventeenth Century Chronicles of Marvara: A Study in the Evolution and Use of Oral Traditions in Western India', *History in Africa*, 3, pp. 127–53 and N. P. Ziegler, 1976, 'Marvari Historical Chronicles: Sources for the Social and Cultural History of Rajasthan', *Indian Economic and Social History Review* 13, pp. 219–50.

tradition bestows on the Meo called Yasin sole authorship of the movement. It does not even register the presence of non-Meo communists who played a significant role in the making of peasant resistance. The other title for *Govindgarh* is *Yasin Khan ki bat*, which indicates Abdul's own point of view. He characterizes it as a *jigar dastan* (a story from the heart). 'In those days there was none who was educated among the Meos. When the Viceroy offered him a chair [position], it meant the death of Rajput rule [*Je mevan ke kursi pari, duba rajputan ka raj*].' The phrase *jigar dastan*, incidentally, puts together two Persian terms and is a clue to the many connections between Indian and Iranian musical traditions. The word *khandan* has two meanings in Persian, reading and singing, suggesting that singing is a more elaborate form of reading poetry. To make poetry more meaningful to an audience the singer uses melody.

The question of why Abdul would be transmitter of a panegyric to a Duhlot Meo was puzzling, especially since I know that Abdul is a Mirasi patronized more by the Daimrot Meo clan. Why this was so became clear to me only recently. His family had been broadly identified with 'Barelwi' Islam or the 'traditionalist' ideology of Islamic practice that includes the veneration of ancestors and sufi saints. Yasin Khan was for Abdul, as for many Meos, not only a political leader but also a *pir* of a saintly lineage as a Sufi *shaykh* and disciple of the Sufi, Miyanji Raj Shah of Sindh, and he had even contested the leadership of M. Ilyas, founder of the Tablighi Jamaat.[5] I asked Abdul of Yasin's status as a pir. 'Later in life, he went wild—it is believed, he became a *wali* (saint),' he responded.

Even with all these limitations, Abdul's singing/telling of *Govindgarh* is a remarkable portrayal of the nature of the Meo encounter with colonial modernity. The narrative has an evocative coding of colonial and princely state authority with the English official appropriately called *hakam* along with the *Nazim* and *thanedar*. The people are the *parja*, a Sanskrit term, but also referred to as the *raiyat*, derived from Urdu-Persian. They are subjects, not citizens, of the Alwar kingdom. There is a similar bi-linguality in the idea of *faraj* (the *farz* of Urdu-Persian or duty) and of the state as responsible for *raja dharma* or moral order. The Badshah is referred to as the ruler of the kingdom of 52 forts invoking the materiality of power. In the narrative Yasin refers to Jai Singh as *rais* (élite personage) rather than raja, donning a

[5] Y. Sikand, 2002, *The Origins and Development of the Tablighi Jamaat (1920–2000): A Cross-country Comparative Study,* New Delhi, Orient Longman, p.147.

turban of Rs 125,000, signifying his worth as *sawai*, the honorary title conferred on the Rajput rulers of the Jaipur State by the Mughals.

In a recent article Rashmi Dube Bhatnagar, Renu Dube and Reena Dube highlight the crisis of bardic traditions under the colonial state that devalued panegyric as sycophancy and was suspicious of orality. They point out the relatively autonomous status of the bard and the pro-woman dissent that the bard was able to proffer vis-à-vis ruling élites despite his dependence on them for patronage.[6] In Abdul's rendering of the narrative of Meo resistance the Rajput queen admonishes the Alwar raja for his injustice to the Meos. In reminding him that the *raiyat* (peasants) are his children she enunciates a moral frame for kingship. The admonishment results in her imprisonment! In chastizing his spouse, Abdul draws an image of a modernizing but highly patriarchal kingship that denies the legitimate protests of its subjects, male and female, Rajput and Meo, royal and peasant.

Abdul is one of the few performers who can take one on a magical journey where existential, lived time recedes into splendorous cosmic time, which is also the time of brotherhood, battle and bloodshed. I travel with Abdul through the epic terrain identified with the Mewati Mahabharata. We follow the Pandavas through their travails: Bhima's confrontation with Hanuman pretending to be an old monkey (in the Sariska National Park), their exile in Bairath (near Jaipur) and their return to claim their right to rule. Draupadi's explicit iconicization as Sakti in the Mewati texts recasts Sanskrit versions of the epic.[7] Although Alf Hiltebeitel has argued that Arjuna and Draupadi in the moment of their disguise as eunuch and maid respectively at the court of the king of Bairath reveal their real identities as Shiva and Shakti.[8] We visit the Lakha mandir at Sainthli/Mina ka bas, the famed Lacquer Palace of the Mahabharata, then drive onto Talbraksha. Is there a secret passage that enabled the Pandavas to escape from the palace while five brahmans and a brahman woman were consumed in its flames? Mina, Gujar and other non-Meo villagers of Sainthli tell a similar story indicating shared inter-communal

[6] Rashmi Dube Bhatnagar, Renu Dube and Reena Dube, 2005, 'A Poetics of Resistance: Investigating the Rhetoric of Bardic Historians of Rajasthan', in Shail Mayaram, M.S.S. Pandian and Ajay Skaria (eds.), *Subaltern Studies* vol. 12, Delhi, Permanent Black.

[7] See S. Mayaram, forthcoming, 'Many Mahabharatas: The Epic Imagination and its (Dis)continuities, in *Text and Variation in the Mahabharata: Regional, Contextual and Performative Traditions*, New Delhi, National Manuscripts Mission.

[8] Alf Hiltebeitel, 1980, 'Siva, the Goddess, and their Disguises of the Pandavas and Draupadi', in *History of Religion*, pp. 147–74.

mythologies. Did Arjuna hide his weapons at Talabraksha, as Abdul claims? Or did this happen in Bairath, as other villagers suggest, highlighting contested cultural memories or, perhaps, a forgetting?

What struck me was the facility with which Abdul could move between what are conventionally regarded as 'Hindu' and 'Islamic' cosmologies. Abdul usually begins his performance with an invocation of the divine, since his art is *kudrat ki den* (the gift of *qudrat* with its range of meanings in Persian including providence, creation, universe, nature). Most often the framing verses that ritualize the performance honor the goddess Bhavani, the Mirasi's *ista devata* (chosen deity), irrespective of whether the narratives are about Hazrat Ali and Nabi Rasul (the Prophet) or about Rama and Ravana.

Pingal is the language of Mewati *kavya*, quite different from Dingal that is the special and secret language of the Charan bards. But the language used by the Meo Mirasis also draws from Persian, Urdu and English and has a predominant flavor of Brajbhasha. For instance, *jamal* (beauty) and *roshan* (luminous) are Persian while words such as *sasrarai* come from Brajbhasha and *paltan* (for platoon) and *bugle* have clear colonial resonances.

Walter Benjamin argues in his 'The storyteller' that the art of storytelling is coming to an end. The storyteller, he elaborates in his marvelous portrait, draws upon the experience that is communicated from mouth to mouth, generation to generation.[9] Abdul, in a sense, embodies both of Benjamin's archaic models of the storyteller: the one who has stayed at home and knows of the local tales and traditions but also the itinerant traveler who goes from place to place. As the latter moves from village to village he carries with him the lore of the community. The nature of the story itself is that it communicates something useful. 'Counsel woven into the fabric of real life is wisdom.' But Benjamin argues, 'The art of storytelling is reaching its end because the epic side of truth, wisdom, is dying out,' displaced by the rise of the novel with printing making possible its dissemination. Storytelling, Benjamin amplifies, is also the art of repeating stories. It derives from the gift of listening, the community of listeners and the possibility of the narrative being integrated into their experience and of their repeating the story to someone else.

Benjamin's work has been extensively used in Benedict Anderson's oft-cited work on nationalism.[10] Had Benjamin been exposed to the

[9] Walter Benjamin, 1992 (1970), *Illuminations,* London: Fontana, pp. 83–86.
[10] B. Anderson, 1983, *Imagined Communities: Reflections on the Origin and Spread of*

non-European experience he would perhaps have come to a different conclusion. The Indian subcontinent has had an extraordinary number of names and caste groups that refer to different dimensions of the storyteller including the *kathakar, sutradhar, kahanikarak, nautanki* and *khyal* performer. Castes such as the Mirasi, Mevon ka Mirasi, Bhat, Charan, Bhand, Dhadhi have been conventional storytellers in addition to certain brahmans, sufis, *mullah*s or Ismai'ili missionaries, *faqir*s, *pir*s, shamans and gurus of all kinds. *Katha*s, *dastan*s, *bhajan*s, *git* and *qawwali*s continue to be important genres used to narrate stories, values and orientations.

Indeed, the role of the storyteller has been reinvigorated as also reinvented in contexts of modernity. Kirin Narayan's ethnography of a Hindu swami brings out the continued power of storytelling in religion.[11] In a fascinating ethnography of an urban center near the border of Pakistan and Afghanistan, Marsden details the way in which performance thrives as resistance to purist Islam but also partakes in an Islamic imaginaire.[12] The Afghan group called 'The Nobles' have produced cassettes more popular than those of Bollywood. Like the Mirasis, their music encodes important ongoing debates among Muslims about Islam and about being a Muslim in the world.

While it is true that oral traditions such as of the Meos are under siege and even the Mewati Mahabharata, the *Pandun ka kara,* is now available on tape, Abdul's neighbors told me on one occasion of their sponsorship of a nightlong performance. Indic epics and Sufi shrines are not just about mythic and mystic universes but have been used to convey development-related messages including literacy campaigns and (inter)nationalism whether Nehruvian, Dravidian Hindutva or Islamist.[13] As new social visions

---

Nationalism, London: (provide the name of the publisher) and B. Anderson, 1998, *The Spectre of Comparisons: Nationalism, Southeast Asia and the World*, London, Verso.

[11] Kiran Narayan, 1992 (1989), *Storytellers, Saints, and Scoundrels: Folk Narrative in Hindu Religious Teaching*, Delhi, Motilal Banarsidas.

[12] M. Marsden, 2002, 'Mahfils and Musicians: New Muslims in Chitral Town, Northern Pakistan', *Occasional Paper No. 5*, Center of South Asian Studies, University of Cambridge.

[13] For an account of a Dhadhi's reshaping of performance aesthetics in line with Akali ideology in the Punjab see M. Nijhawan, 2002, 'Dhadhi Voice and Agency: Performative Genres and the Public Sphere in the Panjab 1920–1935', Draft paper presented to the International Symposium on Folklore, Public Space and Civil Society, Indira Gandhi National Centre for the Arts, New Delhi; also K. Ewing, 1983, 'The Politics of Sufism: Redefining the Saints of Pakistan', *Journal of Asian Studies*, 32, pp. 251–68 for an account of contemporary Sufi shrines in Pakistan.

seek to shape popular religion, Dhadhis and Mirasis continue to innovate and improvize.

Vidiadhar Surajprasad Naipaul in his inaugural address to a meet of literary scholars in India called At Home in the World (Indian Council for Cultural Relations, New Delhi, 2002) spoke about his own experience and learning of literature when he went to England. He contrasted this literary world with the lives of his grandparents from a remote village in India for whom, Naipaul maintained, literature was completely absent. As I heard that address delivered to the high literary establishment in the portals of New Delhi's Vigyan Bhavan, I thought to myself, how little is his understanding of the literary universes that Indian peasants, pastoralists and forest communities have inhabited over the centuries. With Abdul I have traversed realms not accessible to the published world of books, journals and literary magazines—of gods and goddesses along with Ali stories, tyrannical and enlightened Sultans and rajas, valiant heroes and gargantuan heroines, *jinns* and *paris*, prophets and goddesses....

9

Khatij, A Woman from a Kashmiri Mountain Village

APARNA RAO

We stood with our backs to the old water mill, now run by Gulama,[1] her youngest uncle, and facing the remnants of the old wooden bridge that was swept away by the spring floods two years earlier. Khatij and I first met in June 1982 and thereafter for a few months every year till 1990; I met her again briefly in 1994, and then again in 1999; we met for the last time in the summer of 2001, a few months before she died. Over the years we had come to appreciate and like each other—and if I may be allowed an anthropologist's illusions, even grew close to each other. So, when I was invited to write a 'portrait', I instinctively thought of her. I have tried to sketch what she told me of her life, and yet in translating her words, in recalling the time spent together, in recounting her life I have added my voice to hers. I have tried not to foist my interpretations or perspectives, and had it been possible, I would have preferred to enable her to speak alone. For Khatij's was one of the myriad 'unheard voices' of the Kashmir Valley—a voice similar in many ways and yet different in other aspects from the voices which Asiya Geelani was so bravely and sensitively trying to render audible over the last few years.[2]

'Remember how out of breath you used to get when we used to walk up that slope to visit Rahmati?' Khatij asked me with a nearly toothless grin.

---

[1] All personal and most place names have been changed.
[2] This portrait is partly in memory of what Asiya was trying to achieve, and in fond remembrance of Khatij.

Yes, I well remembered those numerous occasions when Khatij took me along on what she referred to as 'going for a walk', when I panted up the slopes with my solid climbing shoes, with her lightly stepping beside or ahead of me, barefoot or with those light cream-colored plastic shoes that most people around here wear. The Rahmati Khatij was referring to was a Poholbai, a professional shepherd woman. Every spring she came up here with her husband and children from their village down below in the valley on their way up to the alpine pastures to which they drove the huge herds of sheep, horses and cows that belonged to the Grishtu, the peasants who spent the whole year still further down where no fodder was left at the end of the long cold winters. In spring and autumn, on their way up and down from their alpine pasture, Rahmati and her family camped for a few weeks each high above Khatij's village, to enable the Grishtu herd owners to reach them more easily and bring them salt for their respective animals. Khatij had never visited Rahmati even higher up, 'right at the top', in the meadow whose name few Grishtu knew, and which Rahmati referred to by its Kashmiri name of 'Yamher' (literally Yama's ladder); Khatij, who was a Gujar,[3] called it by its Gujari name, 'Jamsheri'.

Now, 20 years on, Khatij was too frail and her joints too painful with age and the cold, humid mountain air to swiftly climb those slopes to where Rahmati's camp had been. And 'anyway', she said, 'there's no fun in climbing up there anymore—you can no longer lie in peace in the cool grass and look up at the clouds in the sky...look there is the military, and there, and there—these big burly men are all around, and always ask questions...and Rahmati and her family have stopped coming after old Ahad [Khatij's husband's uncle] and Sheria [Khatij's younger brother] were taken...and then one has to scuttle home so early, because they are also still there—they're above in the forests, above the military and we can't see them, but they can see us and they can see the military and they come when it's dark, and you never know when they'll let off a bomb...no it's best to stay home these days....'

In the village Khatij found little time to talk: in the early days when her husband, Abud, was still alive and well, the fields had to be sown and

---

[3] A large proportion of the population of Jammu and Kashmir consists of Gujar and culturally and historically allied communities, who speak their own language, but are otherwise far from homogeneous, there being several economically and socially distinct and endogamous sections of Gujar in the area. This heterogeneity is possibly explained by different waves of migration and various phases of displacement, followed by attempts at optimising their new ecological and socio-economic adaptation.

harvested in spring and autumn. In summer, after a quick breakfast of salt tea with roasted maize flour (*sattu*), she joined the other women when they went to the forest to collect deadwood and trudge back carrying bundles equal to their own weight on their heads. The logs would be used to cook during the day and stored for use in the long cold winter months when temperatures drop to -20°C and the snow is piled high even on bright sunny days. She helped her step-daughter-in-law, Guli, cook the evening meal and feed the hens and milk the cow. Whenever the time came to send salt up to Ramzan, the Pohol tending their own small flock of sheep in the pasture at Roil, she pounded the glittering pink rock salt that came from Pakistan and was 'cool', unlike the 'hot' Indian sea salt, to send it up with the *Grishtu* who would pass through the village on their way to their own flocks in Ramzan's care. In the mid-1980s, Khatij herself decided to supplement the meagre family income by taking charge, in her turn, of some other sheep belonging to *Grishtu* further down in the valley's rice belt. Later, when her husband Abud fell ill and became bedridden, much of her time was taken up caring for him, and by then, Mokid, her husband's only child by a previous marriage also had two little children to be cared for while their mother, Guli, went out to work in the fields and forest. By the time Abud died, Khatij herself was no longer in good health and stayed at home a lot, but by then, she had also become something of an expert whom other women consulted when they or their children were sick, or when a child was due. In short, in the village, Khatij was always fairly busy, and had little time to reminiscence or talk about herself—except to complain about her deteriorating eyesight, her joint pains and occasionally, her step-daughter-in-law's behavior.

In the 1980s, it was especially on those long 'walks' we had—visiting her friends, such as Rahmati from whom she also bought a little wool; or her brother Sheria and his family from whom she sometimes got buffalo milk and those delicious round pieces of *kileri* cheese; or shortly before *baisakh*, picking the famed black (*trombukuchh*) or white (*batkuchh*) *k?nkuchh* mushrooms usually to sell for precious cash to Sikh or Muslim traders from the district capital, Islamabad[4] (who, in turn would sell them for good money to Pandit middlemen who would resell them at great profit in Delhi), with a few eaten as a rare delicacy or pierced with a needle and strung on a thread to dry for a special winter dinner; or in summer gathering delicious

---

[4] Islamabad here is the capital of the Anantnag district and is not to be confused with the capital of Pakistan.

wild vegetables to cook later in the day or dry for the winter, or *kazoban* flowers whose stems and leaves are boiled and taken by women for period pains; or taking the family's lone milch cow to graze, or simply walking up to sit quietly at the little spring beneath a small boulder nearby that has always been visited on certain Thursdays by a local *faqir* and was set fire to by members of a militant organization in the 1990s—that Khatij told me about her herself. She told me about the mountains and the rivers around us, about the pains and pleasures of people who lived there, about the women and men she liked and disliked; about what it had been like growing up in those pastures, being married in the village, becoming a wife, a mother and a mother-in-law. Hers was the natural expertise that flows from a life that is a struggle for survival, punctuated now and then by little joys and greater sorrows; and it was among others through her that I, over the years, came to acquire the little knowledge that I have about this world that so many stake their everlasting claim to,[5] but so few care to know even little about.

Khatij remembered her father, Jumma, as a very handsome man, but she had little recollection of her mother who had died giving birth to her brother Sheria—'there were no doctors those days and the *pir* could not be brought in time' for the proper amulets, as it was too far. Their father did not remarry for many years, and the two siblings grew up in the care of an aunt, Begum—the wife of their father's second brother. It was a joint agro-pastoral, transhumant household with a few cattle and a little land in the semi-arid belt (inhabited mostly by Gujar) encircling and above *Kashir* ('where the *shali* begins'), the rice-growing vale of Kashmir, just before it rises into the mountains.

Every spring when the fields had been sown with maize and the winter feed for the cattle was gone and they could no longer survive on the meager spring sprouting in the forests close by, Khatij and her family locked up their little house in the village 'below' where they spent the winters and walked 'up' slowly with their cattle and the most essential of belongings for the summer to their mountain home. Both homes were made largely of mud and wood, and no amount of cleaning and weekly clay-plastering helped get rid of the fleas that lived in the interstices. While in winter the animals provided a great

---

[5] Thus, for example, Kashmir as a whole is referred to in official Indian discourse as an inseparable part of its body (*atoot ang*), and in official Pakistani discourse as its jugular vein (*shah rag*), yet no one has till today asked the inhabitants of the area whether they consider themselves as belonging to either body.

deal of the heating by simply living on the ground floor and thus warming the windowless rooms above, in summer they were left out day and night to graze as they pleased; and only pregnant cattle and sick, newborn calves could be taken in and cared for at the back of the living room. As a child, it was great fun riding on the buffalo's back, or racing with her little cousins and Sheria along the streams dotted yellow and pink with spring crocuses. 'Nowadays', Khatij observed, 'there are good roads above the river and you do not need to ford it at any point'; but in those early days, she recalled, 'you had to skirt the river gushing and foaming like milk' with the spring torrents. It was both frightening and wonderful. And at three or four points you had to cross it, 'balancing along slippery logs, unless you wanted to go all the long way the men did with the cattle'. Once she too had walked that long way to help her father with the animals; it was exciting being with him and being responsible—Sheria was too small and was left with the women and children, while she went with her father and his brother and another neighbor. At night they camped—'somewhat as tourists [did]' in the 1980s, though not in tents, just with a thick *pattu*-blanket over one—in a field, owned by her father's friend—a Kashmiri, and a peasant who was happy to get the dung. After the evening meal of *pingi* gruel in the peasant's kitchen and after the men were through with the *hookah* and the peasant women with their snuff (*nas*), her people went out in the cold to spend the night guarding their animals, while she slept next to the peasant women in the kitchen. This was her first night in a Kashmiri home—unfamiliar and somehow scary, but 'who knew that fate had in store for [her] that [she] would be married into a Kashmiri home!' The next day they moved further up to join the rest of the family in their own summer home, not very far from the village Khatij would be married into years later and where we met. Here everything was different from the winter-village below—there was cool water and lush green grass everywhere; one could take the animals and go off in any direction, eat one's fill of sweet-sour berries, sit and plait the long 'bear's grass' into lovely dolls and play to one's heart's content. Even when one was older and had to help gather vegetables and later, even churn milk, life was 'easier and freer up here'. But summers must come to an end and so every autumn Khatij returned with her family to their winter village, where grass was to be cut for winter hay and the crops guarded against bears who came down now to eat the ripening maize cobs.

Khatij never went to school, and could not read or write. But both her father Jumma, who was very pious, and her uncle Gulama who ran the village water-mill in the 1980s, taught her much about the 'sharra' (shariat). She could say her prayers and tell right from wrong, 'knew haram from halal'. She also knew the rites to be performed at a delivery, at birth, at circumcisions, weddings, funerals and burials; she knew how and when to feed the birds when an infant died, what to do when an adult male drowned in a flash flood and risked being swept away to her abode by rantas.[6] She also knew the ceremonies to be performed when young men died suddenly, brutally, as in the firing at Shish Nag; she knew how to apply henna and deck out the sacrificial animal at Eid; she knew the spring ceremonies before the first sowing. She knew the rites for a niaz in summer when it rained long and hard, endangering the harvest, the livestock on the alpine slopes above the village, and the village men who took their horses, sometimes for days on end, accompanying some foreign tourist on a trek or Indian pilgrims to Ambarnath(Amarnath)—both very welcome but somehow alien in this world of ice-framed narrow mountain passes, and ancient wayside shrines that attest to the historical complexity of human faith, a world entirely in Allah's hand and yet peopled also by powerful deo, rantas and wanamohinyu.

When Khatij was about 14 or 15, her aunt Begum who had been looking after the joint household died. It had been a very severe winter, and Begum 'who was always a little weak started coughing up blood and passed away soon after'. Khatij was now the eldest of seven children in the family and 'without an adult woman it was almost impossible to run a pastoral household'. Her father, Jumma, decided that the only way out was to remarry, but he had no money to pay the bridewealth. Around this time a Kashmiri friend of his, Subhan, himself an elderly widower, mentioned that he was looking for a wife for his own son, Abud, who too had become a widower some years earlier. Abud had been left with a young son, Mokid, who was first brought up by his deceased mother's brother in the latter's village, but after a few years returned to Abud in his parental village. Old Subhan was not in good health and wished to see Abud married again before he died. He was far from well-to-do, but was less desperately poor than Jumma, and so the latter suggested that Abud marry Khatij in return for a bridewealth, that was lower than what would have to be paid for a Kashmiri girl, but decent enough for Jumma to find himself a wife—a widow with two young children of her own. It was very unusual for even a

---

[6] Deo, rantas and wanamohinyu (her husband).

poor Gujar girl to be married at this young age to a widower, but both
financial considerations and the fact that Khatij's groom Abud 'had the
reputation of being a very good and hardworking young man' influenced
the decision.

Though Khatij's natal and marital families were both very poor—in
today's administrative jargon 'BPL', 'below the poverty line'—following
custom that still prevail, she was not 'sent' to her husband's family for a few
years; they had to wait till she was physically mature. In the mean time,
however, her father married and brought home his new wife, who like the
stereotypical stepmother was unkind to Khatij. So, 'when the time to be sent'
to her husband came, Khatij was 'happy enough'. But she was sad to leave
behind Sheria and her little cousins, and she was more than apprehensive of
going to live in a Kashmiri village, with only Kashmiris whose language she
still could not speak properly and none of her own Gujar people around.
She didn't think she'd like to 'dress like the young Kashmiri women—with
such a wide and short shirt, without the lovely [tin-and-'silver'] jewellery or
embroidered *topi* and with [her] hair in just two plaits' instead of the
intricately braided way she was used to. Those days, she remembered, the
village women here had just two suits—one very rough and heavily repaired
for everyday wear, and one for festive occasions. 'They were all made of
wool which one got from one's own sheep; it was carded and taken to the
weaver and tailor who turned them into clothes for both men and women.'
Later, she recalled how printed colorful chintz material came in for the
women and cotton cloth for the men. 'When one went out in the cold one
slipped on a woollen *pheran* that one usually shared with other women [in
the household] and that had to last, tatters and all, for two or three years.' By
the 1980s more such woollen *pheran* were available in most households, and
by the late 1990s these were being replaced by synthetic ones tailored from the
produce of Bombay's textile mills. 'Only recently', Khatij remarked with
disdain the last time we met, have 'the young begun to fuss about clothes being
too heavy or itchy—now they want plastic clothes in different colors....'

By 2001, clothes had, definitely become an issue in the village—not just
their quantity and quality, but also their moral significance. An example is
the *burqa*, known here as *chadri*. The first time I saw a *chadri* in this village
was in 1987—years before either the militants or the army were in sight—
when Guli, Khatij's stepdaughter-in-law, brought one back as an Eid present
from her mother's brother, a peasant of some standing in another larger
village. This uncle had two friends who wanted to try their hand at selling

shawls in India in the winter; he had lent them some money as initial capital and in gratitude they had brought him a few Indian presents, including two *chadris*—one of which he gave his daughter, the other his niece. For a few days Guli's new soft and shiny black garment was fingered, unfolded and folded by a series of visiting neighbors' wives, sisters and daughters, and Guli came to be envied and admired for possessing such an apparently rare and prestigious piece of clothing, which was wrapped up carefully and put away, to be worn, I was told, on some special occasion—a wedding outside the village, a hospital visit all the way to the district capital Islamabad, a visit to the shrine below, and so on. Soon, more and more young women wanted to possess such a garment and flaunt it when they went out; and Khatij recounted how since the early-1990s young men returning from the nearest towns would thus often bring back *chadris* as loving presents for their wives and sisters. Almost incidentally, this desire in the village coincided, however, with a change in the wider society, and a few years later, Khatij remembered, how preachers 'from below' would come by and try and 'teach them' that the *chadri*—rather than, or in addition to, their usual colored head scarves—is 'a must for a Muslim woman'. These preachers were 'good men, who helped in many ways', yet even in 2001, though many in this village apparently had a *chadri*, no one actually wore one, except when they left the village to go to town, or to a neighboring village, and then too, it was worn more as a large cloak, with the face left entirely uncovered. 'But why should I hide myself in this black covering, what have I to feel ashamed of?!' exclaimed Khatij; and Phata, a neighbor's wife and a close friend added, 'How can one work wearing such a thing? These men don't know what it is to work!' 'The main thing for everyone—man and woman—', Khatij added, 'is to be decently dressed, not to be naked. We are all decently clothed—we don't dress like those half-naked *sadhs*[7] who go to Ambarnath, or like those *angrez* (foreign) tourists who used to come in the old days. Some of them used to be half naked, and that was not nice, but they kept to themselves far from us and didn't stay long anyway.'

At the time of her marriage, Khatij also disliked the idea of having to eat the thick gruel made from split-*pingi* or buckwheat with milk or buttermilk. She knew she'd badly miss her maize bread, for that was yet to become the staple in her husband's village as it was by the time I came to know it in the 1980s. Neither her people nor her husband's people had ever eaten rice

---

[7] Hindu holy men and mendicants.

(which in its turn is now displacing maize), but had heard of rich people eating it at weddings. She had also rarely eaten potatoes, but here, potatoes boiled and eaten with a little salt and chillies were common. Another novelty was tea, which was drunk then as now with salt and sprinkled with a little roasted maize flour (*sattu*), but made those days from wild strawberry (*tasm*) roots in summer and the bark of the yew tree in winter. She was especially concerned about what would happen in the autumn when all the Gujar from the mountains went down to their villages, leaving her to fend for herself in this new world. There was another girl 'from the mountains' married into this village, a Poholbai, but she too was, after all a 'Koshur'. Although there had been close economic links between Gujar and the villagers for as long as people could remember, at the time Khatij was the only Gujar girl married into this village; since then, there have been a few more such marriages, and Khatij had even heard that in the neighboring village a young man was soon going to marry 'a Bangali girl from far away, from even beyond Punjab'.

In the first few months after her marriage, Khatij would have given a lot to be able to 'go down', back to the village which she had till then found so much less attractive than the mountains up here. But her husband and his father and many people in the village were very kind and understanding and soon Khatij became fluent in Kashmiri and began to get used to the idea of living here permanently and being called 'Khatij' in Kashmiri, rather than 'Khatija', as in Gujri. She was glad not to have a mother-in-law who would dominate her, but sometimes she also felt it would have been nice to have someone older to ask for advice. Her husband's uncle's wife and daughters-in-law lived next door, but after all it was not the same household and one couldn't ask for help so freely. Every spring, on their way up, her father and brother visited her, and over the summer months she visited her old friends and companions in their summer homes. 'The year was divided in a way, between the Gujar in summer and the Kashmiri in winter, and each had its good and bad points.' And over the years, Khatij came to be accepted as a member of the village, and yet remained somewhat of an outsider.

In the 1990s it was hard enough to meet, let alone go for walks beyond the village. Tension with various militant groups, some of whose basic aspirations—freedom and honor ('*azadi*' and '*izzat*')—Khatij and her friends and neighbors had come to share after years of Kashmiri misrule and Indian injustice, but whose violent strategies and domineering behavior they disapproved of and feared; terror of Indian security forces 'whose language we old people don't understand' and whose terrifying uniforms and 'dark and grim faces matched their abusive ways and frequent brutality'; and a general atmosphere of mistrust and unease left little space for normal conversation. So when we met again for the last time in a context of relative relief from the near-daily harassment and brutality of a variety of ubiquitous armed men, and longing for peace and lasting justice, we had much to reminiscence and catch up on. Much had happened in the last 20 years in her personal life.

Her two eldest surviving children (out of six pregnancies)—Arshid and Jamila—whose exchange engagement with another equally poor sibling pair in a neighboring village was being discussed in the late 1980s, had got married with a minimum of expense and turned her into a grandma three times over. She was now on the lookout for a bride for her third and last child, Javed, but felt that he might find a bride in the household he had gone to work for. A *gar-pet* ('live-in-son-in-law') was not what she would have wished him to be, but then 'poor people like us don't have a choice', she observed. Misar, Guli's sister, whose wedding I had attended in 1989, hadn't been happy with her husband and had left him, got a divorce and married someone else. Neither Khatij nor Misar had even heard of the stereotyped '*teen talaq*' (according to which a Muslim man can divorce his wife by saying the word '*talaq*' to her three times) of India. But this wedding was not like other weddings—there was no music, no songs, no dancing, and even the taped Kashmiri songs played by Misar's brother on a borrowed tape recorder were played softly enough for the music not to resound across the village. Khatij recalled with horror the night when 'militants' had broken into their home, smashed Arshid's *rabab* (a stringed musical instrument), beaten him, Javed, Mokid and other men, and raided other homes for drums and stringed instruments. She failed to understand 'why they had done this', why singing such wonderful songs 'in the praise of Allah, of his Prophet, of the great Sheikh Nurdin was wrong'. That night was etched deep in her memory, just like that other night when the military had come with huge searchlights, cordoning off the village, sending its 'armed and booted men into each home to search every nook and corner and trample and tread over everything, including [their] clothes and pots and pans'. But she and the others had retained their presence of mind, and 'When the men were taken out of the houses and lined up outside, we all, all the girls and women also decided to come out; we didn't want to share the fate of other villages, of girls and even elderly women who had remained inside and were raped by these brutes'.

Oh yes, in the last years Khatij had witnessed much trouble. Guli had been ill for quite a while, first after her 'operation', for she and Mokid wanted no more children, and then out of worry when her brother was summoned and kept for days by the 'HM commander' (*Hizb-ul Mujahidin*). Those were the days when the '*tanzeems* were settling disputes and meting out justice in the [institutional] vacuum that was [officially] known as an elected government'. Luckily, the brother-in-law of this commander was also related to someone in Guli's village, and so her brother was released after being reprimanded. Khatij knew what it was like to worry about a brother. She herself had spent many sleepless nights and exhausting days running from pillar to post to find out the whereabouts of her own brother Sheria when he was 'taken away by the military. Of all people, he and old Ahad, [who was half blind, had been] marched off as suspected terrorists, their hands tied behind their backs. No one knew why, till much later', when the village found out that Shafi, another Gujar who had always been inimical to Sheria, and Hassan, a Kashmiri from a neighboring village who had been involved in illicit timber deals, 'had been promised good money by the military if they identified [local] men involved in terrorism'. Ultimately both Sheria and Ahad were released, but 'only after days of torture and confinement'.

Khatij had never been much interested in politics or political parties, but she knew certain names and was well aware of certain issues. In the 1980s, she, like other villagers, had referred with gratitude to 'Bakshi Sab' (i.e., Bakshi Ghulam Mohammad), for having in the past made some basic infrastructural improvements in the area—the first road, the first measures against landslides—and also opened up a few employment opportunities. This notwithstanding, she and her village had never voted for the Congress and were not in favor of it as a party—'it's not our party' she would say. Their party was the 'National' (i.e., the National Conference party) and as such Khatij always remained a follower of 'Sheikh Sab' (i.e., Sheikh Mohammad Abdullah). And in the elections of the early 1980s, she too had voted for 'Sheikh Sab's son, Farooq Sab' (i.e., Farooq Abdullah), since like her neighbors, she too was for community '*izzat*' which was under attack from 'Dilli and Hindustan'. In the late 1980s, she, like all others she knew, had voted for the same reason against Farooq and for the MUF (Muslim United Front). Later still, in an election in the 1990s, she had again voted, but 'only because the military had threatened [them] all with dire consequences if [they] did not'. Following both commonsense and prevailing opinion, Khatij too was convinced that 'the people must be asked to decide about their future; after all, even when deciding on a marriage good parents ask the boy and the girl'.

Like her friends, relatives and neighbors, Khatij was for *azadi*, but she saw no good in the gun, and when there had been talk of the village boys 'going across' for training, she, like most of her generation, had been against it. For her, *azadi* simply seemed 'the only way to attain some prosperity, justice and honor', but it seemed to have nothing to do with Islam, or being a Muslim. 'No one ever asked us not to pray, not to keep *roza* (the ritual fast during Ramzan), not to be a Muslim…', she told me. But then, for Khatij, being a Muslim was an unquestioned way of being. 'It had always been so and why would or could it be otherwise?' 'Only twice' in her life, she recalled, had she 'asked [her] self what a Muslim is': the first was 'when news spread that [an old] temple' close to a neighboring village 'had been attacked by militants in the name of Islam'. The Pandit who took care of it had long fled, but his duties had been taken over by a young Muslim from that village; he too had been threatened to keep away. Thereafter, village 'families took turns and sent their sons every night to guard that temple. After that who would dare attack again!' The second occasion was when the boulder with the little spring in her own village was attacked and set fire to, again 'by militants in the name of Islam'—'that was a sin', she opined; 'how can anyone become a better Muslim by doing such things? After all, it is something which people have revered'. The old *faqir* who came to that place on Thursdays didn't come for a while—'first he was threatened by the militants who said he was not doing what Muslims should do and also because they thought he was a spy for Hindustan; then he was beaten up by the military who thought he was with the militants.' Of late he had started coming again and Khatij and the other village women all gave him little food or money.

In Kashmir's remoter villages, where most people are anyway Muslim, the experience of being a Muslim was till recently not a conscious issue. In the 1980s, Khatij had met only two Pandits, one a doctor, the other a man who worked for some government department and came to the village now and then to check things. In the 1990s she knew that they no longer came and she had heard that they had left, and 'people say that one of their people had been killed and so they had all left for Panjab'. Khatij disapproved of the idea, but seemed to think it best not to talk about it too much, too openly. For Khatij, both in the 1980s and later, communal riots in India, the sacrilege at the Babri Masjid, even the Gujarat pogrom and genocide remained matters of little concern—after all, all those dreadful things happened 'far away, in

Hindustan', and there were so many matters of greater concern right there, in Kashmir. For Khatij, as for her friends, neighbors and relatives, her village was in Kashmir—not in Hindustan, let alone in Bharat, of which she had never even heard.

10

Dr Zakira Ghouse
A Memoir[1]

SYLVIA VATUK

Dr Zakira Ghouse, the woman whose portrait I paint here, passed away in Chennai on the night of 23 January 2003 at the age of 81. As soon as she had breathed her last, her family immediately began telephoning a wide circle of other relatives and friends to inform them of her death. Those who were in Chennai at the time hurried to the house for a final glimpse of the deceased before her burial. Her funeral prayers (*namaz-i janaza*) were recited the following noon at the shrine of Hazrat Dastagir Sahab: the crowd of mourners was so large that many of the men who had gathered at the mosque for the services could not enter and had to pray standing on the steps outside. One of her cousins had gone personally to the office of the *Hindu*, the major English-language newspaper of the city, to submit a brief death notice informing the paper's readers of her demise and announcing the venue where her last rites were to be held. By way of identification, the newspaper piece described Dr Ghouse only as a former lecturer in Urdu at the local Ethiraj Women's

[1] This portrait of Zakira Begum is necessarily partial and limited. It presents her as seen through my eyes, those of a friend and research collaborator from a very different religious and cultural background, whom she came to know only in the last two decades of her life. I have supplemented my own understandings of her life and character by referring to some of her own writings and by consulting her daughter, Rafeth Yasmin, and her younger son, Muhammad Javed, for their insights into their mother's personality and life experiences. I am grateful for their help and for that of her younger sisters, Dr A.M. Nasira and the late A.W. Shakira.

College.[2] She would probably have been pleased to have her formal teaching career publicly acknowledged in this way. But that bare statement hardly does justice to the long life of an intelligent, warm, generous and broad-minded woman, who from her earliest years had striven, against many odds, to get an education and pursue a professional career. To those who knew her she was, in the words of her elder daughter, Rafeth Yasmin, 'a multi-faceted personality, a zealous scholar, a fiery writer and much more!'

At the time of her death Zakira Begum and I had been friends for almost 20 years.[3] We had seen one another most recently in Chennai, shortly before her eightieth birthday. She was then in failing health but mentally very active, still living in her modest house in a neighborhood that is today quite centrally located but at the time of its original settlement was on the outskirts of the then town of Madras.[4] The 8-acre property, occupied by one

[2] http://www.hinduonnet.com/thehindu/2003/01/25/16hdline.htm, accessed on 15 March 2004. More substantive obituaries, highlighting her achievements as a writer and scholar of Urdu, appeared shortly thereafter in Urdu-language newspapers in Hyderabad, the city of her birth, where many close family members still resided.

[3] We had first met in 1984 at the home of her mother, Amat-ul Majid Sakina, in Hyderabad, where I had recently begun a research project on Muslim family and kinship organization that—in large part because of Zakira Begum's inspiration, encouragement and practical assistance—eventually metamorphosed into a history of her own ancestral family (see Sylvia Vatuk, 1989, 'Household Form and Formation: Variability and Social Change among South Indian Muslims', in J.N. Gray and D.J. Mearns (eds.), *Society from the Inside Out: Anthropological Perspectives on the South Asian Household*, New Delhi and London: Sage Publications, pp. 107–39; Sylvia Vatuk, 1990, 'The Cultural Construction of Shared Identity: A South Indian Muslim Family History', in P. Werbner (ed.), *Person, Myth and Society in South Asian Islam*, Special Issue, *Social Analysis* 28, pp. 114–31; Sylvia Vatuk, 1994, 'Schooling for What? The Cultural and Social Context of Women's Education in a South Indian Muslim Family', in C.C. Mukhopadhyay and S. Seymour (eds.), *Women, Education, and Family Structure in India*, Boulder: Westview Press, pp. 135–64; Sylvia Vatuk, 1997, '"Learning for the Glory of God" vs. "Useful Knowledge": Muslim Scholars Confront the Spread of Western Schooling in Nineteenth Century Madras', Unpublished paper presented at the 49th Annual Meeting of the Association for Asian Studies, Chicago; Sylvia Vatuk, 1999, 'Family Biographies as Sources for an Historical Anthropology of Muslim Women's Lives in Nineteenth-century South India', in J. Assayag (ed.), *The Resources of History: Tradition, Narration and Nation in South Asia*, Paris and Pondicherry: Institut français, pp. 153–72; and Sylvia Vatuk, 2004, '"*Hamara Daur-i Hayat*." An Indian Muslim Woman Writes her Life', in David Arnold and Stuart Blackburn (eds.), *Telling Lives in India: Biography, Autobiography, and the Life History*, New Delhi: Permanent Black and Bloomington: Indiana University Press, pp. 144–74.

[4] Since during most of Zakira Begum's lifetime the city was officially known as Madras, I will henceforth refer to it by that name.

substantial two-storey house and several out-buildings, had been purchased in 1863 by one of her great-great-grandfathers, the former Diwan of the Carnatic, to house his family and that of his recently deceased younger brother. Over the years many more houses were constructed and eventually a small mosque with adjoining *madrasah* and a library to house family members' extensive collections of old Arabic, Persian and Urdu manuscripts and books were added. Today even the interior portions of the original property are almost entirely built upon and the fruit trees and pond that once graced it are long gone. But the locality is still known, at least by local Muslims, as 'The Diwan's Garden' (*diwan sahab bagh*). Virtually all of the original land remains in family hands and many of the Diwan's descendants still live there.[5] But many rent out portions of their holdings to outsiders, so the *bagh* is no longer the exclusive family compound that it once was.

Zakira Begum had lived in Diwan's Garden since 1954. She had been born and raised in Hyderabad, in a large, close-knit, religious and scholarly extended family (*khandan*) of the Nawwayat community (*qaum*). The Nawwayats are Sunni Muslims of the Shafi'i school of law, found in relatively small numbers but widely dispersed throughout southern India. They trace their ancestry to Arab seafarers who settled in the vicinity of Goa, probably in the mid-fourteenth century. Zakira Begum's own ancestors included many religious scholars (*ulema*) who served in judicial and administrative positions in the sultanates of Bijapur and Bidar and under the later Mughal rulers of the Deccan. From the mid-eighteenth century they were associated with the Nawabs of the Carnatic, first in Arcot and later in Madras. In 1801, a prominent ancestor was appointed Diwan in Nawab 'Azim-ud Daula's court. In time his elder son succeeded him, the younger became Chief Qazi and several of his grandsons also received Nawabi appointments. But when Nawab Ghulam Ghaus Khan died without issue in 1855 the British refused to recognize a successor, pensioned off his higher-ranking officials and dismissed the others. Their livelihood gone or greatly reduced, some of the younger men of the *khandan* left Madras for Hyderabad to find employment. Their descendants formed the nucleus of a new branch of the *khandan* in that city. By the 1920s, most of Zakira Begum's relatives in both cities were

[5] According to a household census of the *khandan* (family) conducted under my direction in 1984, there were approximately 300 descendants of the former Diwan and his siblings still living in Madras, all but a handful in Diwan's Garden; see Vatuk, 1989, 'Household Form and Formation'.

people of relatively modest means, though still highly respected in the local Muslim community for their learning and probity.

For generations, most marriages in the *khandan* joined cousins or other close relatives.[6] Zakira Begum's parents were doubly first cousins: their mothers were sisters, their fathers were brothers and two of their grandparents were siblings as well. Her parents married in 1912, when she was 14 and he was 19. Shortly after their marriage they spent several years in Mecca, where his father had gone into exile after being banished by the then Nizam Mahbub 'Ali Khan, on being falsely accused of participating in a plot against him. In Mecca Zakira Begum's mother gave birth to a stillborn daughter and a year later another newborn, who lived for only a day. The couple returned to Hyderabad when Zakira Begum's grandfather was cleared of the conspiracy charge and there her mother conceived again. Everyone's hopes were focussed on ensuring this child's survival. Extra care was taken of the expectant mother and many prayers were offered. Zakira Begum was welcomed into the world with much joy, not only by her parents but by her entire extended family

The four-generation household in which Zakira Begum spent her early years included her paternal grandparents, three of their sons with their wives and children and the spouses and children of some of the latter as well. Her grandfather was then employed in the Translation Department (*dar-ut tarjuma*) of Osmania University, in charge of ensuring that books being translated from English into Urdu for classroom use contained no religiously objectionable material.[7] Her uncles worked in other government offices. Her father was still studying, working toward a B.A. degree at Osmania University, the first in the family to attempt such a course of study. But, despite his educational qualifications, his erudition and his literary talents, he was for many years unable to secure a permanent job and worked only intermittently in short-term, temporary posts. One of his jobs was as assistant to the compiler of an English-Urdu dictionary that became a

---

[6] Occasionally a couple was only distantly related or even unrelated but the incoming spouse was almost always a Nawwayat. In a very few cases a *khandan* man whose first wife had died married, of his own choice, a woman from another Muslim *qaum* or even a Hindu convert (a so-called *naumuslim*, 'new Muslim').

[7] Osmania University, the first modern university to employ Urdu as the medium of instruction, began operating in 1918. The university's Translation Department rendered hundreds of standard English scientific and humanities works from English into Urdu for use as texts.

standard reference work.[8] But eventually he decided to go into business, setting up a commercial lending library, the first of its kind in Hyderabad. His wife offered all her jewellery for conversion into cash, providing the initial capital for this venture.

He ran the library for many years out of rented premises[9] but throughout most of Zakira Begum's childhood his income was insufficient for his family's needs and he and his wife and children—eventually three daughters and a son—relied heavily upon the earnings of his father and older brothers.[10] In her memoirs[11] Zakira Begum writes that their precarious economic situation and their dependence on others for support distressed her mother greatly. She communicated these feelings to her children in a variety of direct and indirect ways, often impressing upon them the need to behave in a self-effacing manner and avoid making any demands for luxuries beyond their minimum requirements for food and shelter. Thus, from an early age, Zakira Begum was made conscious that they occupied the position of 'poor relations' within the household. She wished that she and her sisters and brother could have all of the things that other children in the extended family took for granted but knew that they must not ask for them. She suffered greatly from feelings of deprivation and neglect but, rather than simply accept the situation as her fate in life, made up her mind to change it. She determined to make something of herself, to earn the respect of others by noteworthy and exceptional accomplishments that would bring not only honor but financial stability to her and her family.

In the sprawling one-storey house in which she grew up, each married couple and their minor children occupied one or two rooms, all arranged

[8] 'Abdul Haq, 1937, *The Standard English-Urdu Dictionary*, Silsilah-i Matbu'at-i Anjuman Taraqqi-i Urdu, No. 106, Aurangabad: Anjuman-i Urdu Press. 'Abdul Haq, the author of this dictionary and other linguistic and literary works, served for a time as Head of the Osmania University Translation Department. Zakira Begum later wrote a biography of the man; see Zakira Ghouse, 1975, *Hayat-i Haq: 'Abdul Haq ki Zindagi ki Chand Jhalkiyan*, Madras: Model Art Press.

[9] After his death in 1944, one of his daughters, Amat-ul Wahab Shakira, took over its management. She later trained as a professional librarian and worked for many years in the Osmania University Library.

[10] Their situation was aggravated by the fact that he had by then taken a second wife and had two more daughters by her. They lived in a separate residence.

[11] This unpublished memoir, *Hamara Daur-i Hayat*, was written in a series of chapters in the early 1950s for a family audience. It covers the first 12 or so years of her life, with a later addendum describing her early years of marriage and childbearing; see Vatuk, 2004, "*Hamara Daur-i Hayat*".

around open courtyards. There was a single kitchen: the women of the family shared the responsibility of meal planning and preparation while female servants handled the heavier household chores. Usually one woman was in charge of deciding what would be cooked each day, organizing the work to be done by her sisters-in-law and nieces, supervising the servants, seeing to it that the meals were ready on time and dishing out the portions, so as to make sure that everyone present was adequately fed and there was sufficient food remaining for anyone who returned home late.

The women practised strict seclusion (*gosha*) from unrelated men and had little contact even with women of other families. Men took care of the shopping and any other tasks requiring contact with the outside world. But women did have opportunities to visit relatives elsewhere in the city for weddings, birth and death ceremonies and the many calendrical observances of the Muslim ritual year. There were also frequent trips to visit family members in Madras or in one of the district towns where some men of the *khandan* were posted in connection with their government employment. Aside from the pilgrimage to Mecca—which many women of the *khandan*, even in the nineteenth century, had performed at least once in their lifetime— it had become increasingly common for groups of women and girls, always accompanied by a few men and boys, to visit the shrines of Muslim saints in the vicinity of Hyderabad or Madras and even further afield. Often these pilgrimages were combined with visits to famous tourist sites, to museums, parks, beaches and other places of interest and amusement.

Whenever women left the home, they travelled in curtained vehicles: horse- or bullock-drawn carts or rickshaws. On trains they rode in the women's compartment. As in other 'respectable' (*sharif*) families, whenever women boarded or alighted from a vehicle servants held up broad lengths of opaque fabric on either side of the doorway of the building they were entering to shield them from the sight of strangers. Later women began instead to wear the *burqa*, a garment that fully covered the face and body and allowed greater freedom of movement through public spaces.

In her memoir, Zakira Begum describes the atmosphere of her childhood home as dominated by religious worship and by intellectual and scholarly activities. Everyone took part in the prescribed daily prayers and scrupulously observed the rules of fasting and almsgiving (*zakat*) during Ramzan. They regularly gathered to hear one of the more religiously knowledgeable men recite passages of the Quran aloud—often from memory, a highly valued accomplishment that several had achieved—and expound upon their meaning. Stories about the Prophet and his family and companions were regularly narrated, providing models of exemplary behavior for adults as well as children to emulate.

The men of the family were also very much interested and involved in what was going on in the wider world, keeping up with current events by reading newspapers, attending public lectures and gathering for discussions with colleagues and friends. Several uncles and older cousins wrote for local newspapers and other Urdu-language publications. Some belonged to voluntary associations in the city, where social and political issues were discussed and proposals made for improving the lot of Muslims and advancing conditions in the city at large. They brought new civic society concepts into the home, forming a family 'literary society' (*bazm-i adab*) that held regular meetings to which male relatives living elsewhere in the city were also invited. There they delivered speeches and debated topics of current interest. They wrote articles on a wide variety of religious, political, social and historical (including family-historical) topics, collecting them together each month and distributing them in the form of a handwritten 'magazine' among the various households of the *khandan* in Hyderabad and then sending them to be read by relatives in Madras. Some younger men also organized a club for the family's children, sponsoring speech competitions and debates and giving instruction in essay writing.

In the early 1920s some young women of the family decided to form a similar society for themselves. Though it did not survive for long, its founders being too busy with marriage and children to continue its activities, Zakira Begum remembered sitting in on some of their meetings when she was very young. Seeing these women stand up in front of an audience and express their opinions on various matters made a deep impression on her. So when she was in her mid-teens she sought the cooperation of her young sister and one of her cousins to revive this women's society. They began holding regular meetings in which they took turns delivering speeches. They also began producing a monthly women's magazine *Mushir-un Niswan*, 'The Woman's Advisor'. It was modeled upon the men's family magazine but also drew for inspiration from some of the popular Urdu women's journals being published at the time.[12] Many family members—mostly female but including some males—and a few outsiders contributed to it. It came out on

[12] Gail Minault, 1998, 'Women's Magazines in Urdu as Sources for Muslim Social History', *Indian Journal of Gender Studies*, 5, pp. 201–13.

a more or less monthly basis for almost 25 years and was again briefly revived in the 1970s. Like the men's magazine, it was circulated around the various households of the *khandan*, first in Hyderabad and then in Madras. But Zakira Begum was very careful to retrieve each copy after it had been read and kept every issue right up to the day of her death. They remain in her room to this day, neatly stacked in chronological order. Among other things, this magazine served as a literary training ground for a number of girls who later began submitting articles and stories to local and national magazines and newspapers. Zakira Begum herself began writing for publication when in her late teens and continued to do so throughout much of her life.

Members of the *khandan* had always placed a great deal of value upon learning, stressing in particular the acquisition of religious knowledge and training in the traditional Islamic sciences. Their nineteenth-century ancestors had not only been very negatively impacted economically by the abolition of the Carnatic Nawabi but felt their religious, cultural and linguistic traditions were severely threatened by the rapid spread of the English language and the growing influence of the new forms of knowledge transmitted through it. For several decades, therefore, the *khandan* elders adamantly refused to allow their children to learn English or attend Western-style schools. Like their ancestors, they educated their children at home, following a traditional Islamic curriculum.[13]

The *khandan* had a long tradition of educating girls as well as boys.[14] Children began their formal religious studies with the *bismillah* ceremony, ideally held at the age of four years, four months and four days. They first learned to recognize the Arabic letters in order to 'read', though not necessarily to understand, the Quran. Later they were taught to read and write Urdu, the formal literary language of which their mother tongue, Dakhani, was the local dialect. Most boys and any girls who displayed a particular interest and ability were also taught Persian, used in Madras well into the nineteenth century for official and literary purposes. Some continued on to study Arabic as well.

Zakira Begum was taught to read the Quran by her paternal and maternal grandmothers. She learned Urdu and later Persian from her mother, who also passed on to her daughters her love of reading. Zakira

---

[13] See Vatuk, 1997, "'Learning for the Glory of God'".
[14] Vatuk, 1994, 'Schooling for What?'

Begum soon became a voracious reader and, although she sometimes had difficulty acquiring enough books to satisfy her passion, she read very widely in the Urdu literature that was available to her at the time. She especially enjoyed the women's magazines that sometimes came into the home, either by subscription or borrowed from relatives. She devoured contemporary novels, especially those written for a female audience, and often identified with and tried to model herself upon certain admirable female characters, particularly those who were well-educated in the 'modern' way while also retaining the virtues of the ideal Muslim wife.

One book that she read many times featured a Muslim 'lady-doctor'.[15] Her admiration for this fictional character was reinforced by encounters with a female Christian (probably Anglo-Indian) medical practitioner who was regularly called to the house when a child was to be born. But an even earlier incident may have provided the initial impetus for her medical ambitions. According to family lore, her father had given her a copy book in which to practise writing. In the front he had written the sentence 'I shall study medicine'. Zakira Begum was never quite sure what had impelled him to write this, since in later years he had never orally expressed such an ambition for her and indeed had not begun sending her to school until she was well beyond the age at which children were normally enrolled. But whatever his motivation, that sentence apparently ignited a spark in her mind that continued to burn for many years thereafter. She abandoned the dream it provoked only years later, when it became clear that she would not be able to succeed in the high-school science track that was a prerequisite for entrance into medical college.

By the end of the nineteenth century, the *khandan's* opposition to Western-style education had begun to weaken, at least in some quarters. Zakira Begum's father and a number of other young men of his generation attended English-medium schools. But the idea of formal schooling for girls was slower to gain acceptance. Many feared the consequences of allowing their daughters to come into contact with girls who had not been brought up with the strict moral standards they themselves adhered to. They believed that girls exposed to 'modern' ideas were unfit for domestic duties, dressed and behaved immodestly, turned away from the practice of their religion and refused to defer to their elders and husbands-to-be. By the time Zakira Begum reached

---

[15] Afzal 'Ali, [Walida-i] Muhammad, 1981 [orig. 1911–12], *Gudar ka Lal*, Lucknow: Nasim Book Depot.

school-going age, more than 80 *khandan* boys had received some kind of formal schooling but only two girls had ever set foot inside a classroom. Around this time, however, the parents of two other little girls living in Hyderabad—one of them a first cousin of Zakira Begum's who lived in the same household—enrolled their daughters in an English-medium girls' school.[16] This was a controversial move but the girls' parents refused to yield to family criticism. Zakira Begum writes that for years, every time she saw her younger cousin leaving for school in the morning, she would be overcome with yearning to accompany her. Finally, when she was 12 years old, her father had her admitted to the same school. She was overjoyed, but once there, she was embarrassed and somewhat ashamed to find herself sitting in the second grade alongside many much younger girls Since she knew no English, had studied little arithmetic and had had no exposure to any of the other subjects in the curriculum, there was no question of her being placed in a more age-appropriate class. Ultimately even the second-grade work proved too difficult for her to handle and the following year she transferred to an Urdu-medium school. There she did well and even, by studying on her own outside of class, succeeded in passing her middle-school examination two years early.

During Zakira Begum's childhood she spent several extended periods visiting relatives in Diwan's Garden in Madras. There she came to know a more distant cousin, seven years older than she, who had been born and brought up in Diwan's Garden. Muhammad Ghouse's father had died young but his mother, despite having been left with few financial resources, had somehow managed to raise her children and educate them well. After finishing high school, Ghouse Basha, as he was known, went to Hyderabad for further studies. There he became a regular visitor to Zakira Begum's home. By then, her parents were living separately from the rest of the joint family. Whereas in most families unmarried girls were made to stay out of sight whenever a potentially marriageable male relative came calling, Zakira Begum's parents were somewhat less strict on this point.[17] After a time,

[16] Nampally Zenana School, founded in 1887 specifically to cater to the needs of *goshanashin* girls of élite Muslim and Hindu families.

[17] Islamic law divides relatives of the opposite sex into two categories, *maharam* and *namaharam*. A woman may interact freely with men in the former category, none of whom she may marry. They include her father, uncle, grandfather, son, grandson, nephew and brother. All other male relatives are *namaharam*: they are all regarded as possible spouses. Even if they live in the same household, in many families unmarried *namaharam* are expected to avoid face-to-face contact and are never permitted to be alone with one another.

finding that she needed help with her schoolwork, Ghouse Basha offered to tutor her. In this way the two had an opportunity to become acquainted with one another. Once he completed his B.A. degree and obtained a government job, he asked her parents for her hand in marriage.

There was little precedent in the *khandan* for a young man to independently choose his own wife. Parents were expected to take the initiative in such matters and usually neither of the young people involved was given much of a role in the process.[18] It was always hoped that, once married, a husband and wife would learn to love one another. But romantic attraction was not considered a solid ground on which to base the choice of a life's partner. However, Ghouse Basha's father was deceased and he was already in his early thirties and financially independent, which gave him a certain amount of freedom to act on his own behalf.

When the proposal came, Zakira Begum's father had very recently passed away and her mother was struggling with the problem of how to survive financially with two children still in school, another in college. Her eldest was already 24 years old and still not spoken for at an age when most girls of the *khandan* were already married and some had children of their own. The proposal would seem to have been an attractive one in many respects. The prospective groom was eminently eligible—well-educated, securely employed, closely related and of an appropriate age. He was also handsome and of an agreeable temperament, though these factors would admittedly have been of greater importance to Zakira Begum than to her mother. She would later tell her children that people used to call their father a 'Roman God' because of his good looks and his winning personality. She gave them to understand that she felt very lucky that he had chosen her to be his wife. But, for whatever reason, her mother was initially quite reluctant to give her consent to the match. Other members of the family intervened, urging her to reconsider, and the two were married in July 1944.

Throughout their married life, Muhammad Ghouse's employment as an officer in the Excise Department made him subject to frequent transfers. He had to move from one district town or village to another, in some of which the physical and social conditions were quite harsh and the facilities rudimentary. But his position entitled him to have subordinates who, in

[18] Family lore does record a few previous examples of unmarried young men who set their heart on marrying a particular cousin or other relative. But their elders invariably had the last word. In some cases they agreed to the match and the couple lived happily ever after. In others they insisted that their son marry a girl of their own choice.

addition to their office duties, were available to cook for the family and help his wife with other household tasks and with childcare, giving her considerable time to devote to the reading and writing that were her main passions in life.

Altogether she gave birth to four children, two sons and two daughters. At times she and her children spent extended periods in her natal home, sometimes for health reasons or because her husband's current posting had no accommodations for families, but at other times because she desired to continue her education and found it impossible to do so while living in the countryside. Given her growing family and the requirements of female seclusion, there was no question of trying to enrol as a regular college student. The alternative was to study 'privately', reading the required texts at home in preparation for the periodically scheduled examinations. In order to be able to concentrate more fully on her studies, she often found it necessary to go home to Hyderabad and impose upon her mother's and sisters' willingness to care for her children.

Zakira Begum was fortunate that her husband was supportive of her educational ambitions. Since a respectable woman could not go out of the house alone to visit the various offices where forms had to be filed and fees paid to register as a private examination candidate, he took care of these errands. He suffered without complaint the considerable inconvenience of living alone in distant out-of-the-way places for periods of varying length while she pursued her academic ambitions. But Zakira Begum writes that she was nevertheless under considerable emotional stress in those years, fearing that she might be unable to achieve the academic and career goals she had set for herself. At times the future seemed bleak. Would she never have a life apart from the life of a housewife and mother? While these roles provided her considerable satisfaction, they did not suffice for someone whose dream was to become an accomplished professional woman and to be widely respected beyond the narrow confines of her home and family. She was already in her early thirties and time seemed to be slipping away from her. She desperately wanted to achieve something 'meaningful'. Having long since given up the idea of becoming a doctor, her sights were now set on a teaching career.

She passed her B.A. in January 1952 and went to Nagpur for two weeks with an older male relative to take her M.A. exam the following March. There had been a last-minute crisis when all three children came down with chickenpox shortly before her scheduled departure. But her husband and siblings stepped into the breach, enabling her to go as planned. In June she learned that she had passed, the first woman of her *khandan* to complete a post-graduate degree course. Then she began looking for work. Her initial forays into the job market were unsuccessful, but soon, through contacts made through an acquaintance of her younger sister, she was granted an interview and then offered a job as Urdu lecturer at Ethiraj Women's College in Madras. To accept it would, of course, require moving to Madras. Though her husband was not in a position to accompany her, he accommodated her desire to go. He may have felt that it would be better for the children to live in Madras than for the family to continue to follow him from one rural post to another, particularly now that the two older children, both boys, were of school-going age. In the district town where they had been living, the younger boy had disliked the local school intensely and had sometimes played truant. But it would mean separation from the family for lengthy periods, seeing them only on holidays and whenever he could take leave from his own job. No woman of the *khandan* had ever taken up a job that involved moving far away from her husband's place of work. In fact, for a married woman to enter the workforce at all was almost unprecedented in their *khandan*. An entry in her mother's diary for 20 July 1953—the day Zakira Begum first reported for duty at Ethiraj College—conveys some sense of how her decision to take the job must have been received. Her mother writes: 'for economic reasons, she had to accept this job. Otherwise it would be best for her to serve her husband and take care of her children.' In reality, as we have seen, Zakira Begum's motives for taking a teaching position were not primarily economic. But it was clearly difficult for someone of her mother's generation to grasp the notion that a woman with a husband and small children whose family was not in considerable financial distress would make such a choice.

Ghouse Basha took long leave from his post in order to accompany Zakira Begum and the children to Madras. He enrolled the boys in an Urdu-medium school and for the first month took them to school every day and stayed with the younger one so that he would become accustomed to regular attendance. During this time he also tried to encourage Zakira Begum to work on improving her English, bringing her things to read and urging her to spend some time each day in the effort. The family moved into a house in Diwan's Garden called Bara Ghar ('Big House') that had been left in a family trust (*waqf*) by his late grandmother. His mother and his sister's family, along with some other relatives, were also living there. Unlike the extended household in which Zakira Begum had grown up, here each resident family managed its own cooking and covered its own household expenses. Internal passages connected Bara Ghar with several other adjoining houses, so that residents could visit one another without going outside, a particular convenience for *gosha*-observing women. Here Zakira Begum had the help and support of a close-knit group of nearby kinswomen and was also able to employ servants to take care of household chores and stay with her children while she was at work.

She taught at the college for more than 10 years and would have continued much longer had the institution not decided, in 1965, to eliminate the Urdu-language program and terminate her services. The women of her extended family kept strict *gosha*. Even within the *bagh* they did not venture out of doors without donning a *burqa* and in the beginning she followed the same practice, as she had always done in the past. In the beginning she traveled to work in a rickshaw, hand-drawn by neighborhood men known to the family. She and her two sons would start out together in the morning: first the boys would be dropped off at their school, then she would be delivered to the college, several miles away. But it was not always convenient and was somewhat costly to commute to work this way. Finally her husband made the suggestion, quite radical for the time, that she use the public bus. On one of his periodic visits to Madras he accompanied her to the college several times to accustom her to the route. Thereafter she began traveling on her own. She found it inconvenient to wear a *burqa* on the bus and so discarded it. Some of her relatives were scandalized by her daring and, for a long time, whenever she would encounter certain men in the neighborhood she was overcome by extreme embarrassment. But she gradually conquered these feelings and never wore the *burqa* thereafter, though she always covered her head with the end of her sari when in public.

Zakira Begum obtained a great deal of satisfaction from her teaching career. Aside from the pleasure of the work itself, she welcomed the opportunity to broaden her horizons by seeing other parts of the city that she had never visited before, learning first-hand about the world outside of her home and making new social contacts. She especially revelled in getting to know colleagues and students of other backgrounds and religions, going to their homes, attending their celebrations and visiting their places of worship. Her curiosity about and openness to other people and to different ways of life and thought was something that she credited to her mother's influence. Despite the narrow confines within which her mother had lived her own life, Zakira Begum remembered her as an exceptionally broad-minded and tolerant woman whose example she was pleased to follow and to pass on to her own sons and daughters in turn.

Even after her teaching position was terminated Zakira Begum remained in Madras, in large part in order not to interrupt the education of their children—another daughter had been born in the meantime and all four were in school. Her husband retired and rejoined the family in Madras in the early 1970s. He had earlier purchased a small plot of land in Diwan's Garden from a relative and used some salary arrears that were due to his wife for constructing the house in which Zakira Begum spent the later years of her life. But for many years, instead of living in it themselves, they rented it out to supplement their income. When Ghouse Basha retired, he invested his retirement benefits in the repair of another house located nearby and the family shifted there. Only after his death was Zakira Begum able to evict the sitting tenants who had long refused to vacate her own house, so that she and her daughter's family could occupy it themselves.

Zakira Begum continued to pursue her academic interests. She enrolled in Madras University for an M.Litt. degree and submitted a thesis in 1973 dealing with a prominent eighteenth-century Deccan literary figure named Baqir Aga, a collateral relative of one of her great-great-great-grandmothers, who had also been associated with the Carnatic court.[19] Because of her limited English competence, she wrote the thesis in Urdu and then translated it, with considerable assistance from her husband. Years later, because she wished so ardently to see this work in print, her adult children contributed funds for private publication of the Urdu version.[20]

In 1975, Zakira Begum and her husband were able to fulfill the duty and desire of every observant Muslim to make the pilgrimage to Mecca. On their return they married off both of their sons; their elder daughter had married about eight years prior to this, the younger was still a student. But Ghouse Basha passed away less than three years later, in 1978. Zakira Begum fell into a deep depression after this blow and began to suffer debilitating physical symptoms from which she never fully recovered. During this period she arranged a marriage for her younger daughter with a relative living in

---

[19] Zakira Ghouse, 1973, *Baquir Agah's Contribution to Arabic, Persian and Urdu Literatures*, Unpublished M.Litt. thesis, University of Madras.

[20] Zakira Ghouse, 1995, *Maulana Baqir Aga Veluri: Shakhsiyat aur Fan*, Madras: Tamilnadu Urdu Publications.

Hyderabad. Both sons were now working as engineers in Saudi Arabia and their wives and children were with them. Only her elder daughter remained in Madras. When her son-in-law's ancestral home in *diwan sahab bagh* became available, her daughter suggested that they all move into more spacious and comfortable quarters there. But Zakira Begum was unwilling to do this[21] and her daughter was equally unwilling to move out herself and leave her mother behind. So she and her husband stayed on and raised their three children in Zakira Begum's much smaller house and for several years used his house only as a place to hold private tutoring classes in English, the subject in which her daughter had earned B.A. and M.A. degrees.

Zakira Begum was still not satisfied to sit back and enjoy the blessings of old age. She was thinking about what she should do for the rest of her life. She applied to the Department of Urdu at Madras University, proposing to write a dissertation on the literary, educational and religious accomplishments of the women of her ancestral *khandan*. But she was turned down, probably, at least in part, because of her age. She persisted, however, enlisting influential acquaintances to intervene on her behalf, and eventually gained admission. She wrote the dissertation in Urdu and in 1994, at 73 years of age, was finally awarded her doctorate.[22]

As can be discerned from the foregoing account of her life, Zakira Begum was a strong-willed woman, who from an early age had definite goals in life and almost singlemindedly pursued them, even at the cost of her own comfort and, on occasion, the comfort of other family members. At the same time, she was emotionally fragile and easily hurt; those close to her, especially her husband and children, not wishing to upset her or cause her pain, tended to treat her gently and gratify her wishes to the extent possible. As an adult, she had little or no interest in material things—other than books and papers and things she had written. One of her greatest desires was to see her work in print; she would prefer to spend money for that purpose than for any other. She cared very little about her dress or even about her overall physical appearance. As she wryly admits in her memoir, it had been evident ever since her childhood that neatness was not one of her

[21] It is not customary and indeed is regarded as somewhat shameful for a woman to depend upon a son-in-law for support and even more so to live in his home. This may help to explain Zakira Begum's reluctance to move into a house that belonged to her daughter's husband, notwithstanding its superior material comforts.

[22] Zakira Ghouse, 1994, *Khuwatin-i Khanwada-i Badr-ud Daula ki Adabi, Talimi aur Mazhabi Khidmat,* Unpublished Ph.D. dissertation, Madras University.

virtues! Similarly, she had no interest in or capability for the domestic arts, such as cooking, sewing and embroidery and household management skills that most girls were taught from an early age but that she claimed to have managed to avoid learning properly. She was fortunate in that throughout her adult life; even though her family was by no means well-to-do, she always had at least one servant to do the cooking and other household chores. And her older daughter, once she grew up, took over the responsibility for managing the household they shared and keeping the house in order, so that her mother would not have to concern herself with those matters that she so disliked and could pursue her own interests.

What Zakira Begum enjoyed most of all was to read and to write and to teach others. Even after Ethiraj College dismissed her, she continued to tutor children and young people who would come to her home for help with their Urdu lessons or to get assistance in writing essays or speeches in Urdu for school competitions. She also gave a great deal of time to visiting scholars like myself—I was not the only one with whom she sat for hours reading aloud and explaining texts that we could not easily decipher and hunting for sources that we could use in our research. And she was one of the last people in the *khandan* to take a serious interest in the preservation of its own historical archives, some kept in her own and others' homes, some in the several family libraries still extant in Madras and Hyderabad.[23]

It was a source of extreme sorrow for Zakira Begum that the language to which she had devoted so much of her life and effort was rapidly falling into disuse, not only in India as a whole and in Tamilnadu in particular but even in her own *khandan*, whose children were attending English-medium schools where the only other modern languages taught were Hindi and Tamil or Telugu. Many of these children, while continuing to speak Dakhani at home, did not learn to read and write Urdu well, if at all, and certainly knew little or nothing of the rich literary heritage of the language that had meant so much

[23] See Muhammad Ghouse (ed.), 1968, *A Catalogue of Arabic Manuscripts*, Hyderabad: Sayeedia Library Association; Muhammad Ghouse, 1988, *Kutub Khana-i Rahmaniya, Madras, Tamilnadu, ke Urdu Makhtutat*, Madras: Madrasa Muhammadi; Muhammad Ghouse and Muhammad Afzaluddin Iqbal, 1989, *Amanati Kutub Khana_Khandan-i Sharf-ul Mulk, Madras ke Urdu Makhtutat*, Madras: Madrasa Muhammadi; and Muhammad Ghouse and Muhammad Afzaluddin Iqbal, 1989, *Shams-ul 'Ulama Qazi 'Ubaidullah Oriyantal Laibreri, Madras ke Urdu Makhtutat*, Madras: Madrasa Muhammadi. Note that the author of the cited works is not Zakira Begum's husband but another cousin of the same name.

to her. When these young people went away to America or the Middle East, as so many now did, they were unable to correspond by letter with members of the older generation. Their parents and grandparents had instead to be satisfied with the weekly or bi-weekly telephone call—hardly, in their view, an adequate substitute.

By the fall of 2001 Zakira Begum's domestic situation had changed quite drastically. Both daughters had joined their elder brother in Saudi Arabia and were now employed there. The other son had migrated to Canada with his family. Her granddaughter and one of the grandsons who had grown up in her Madras house were also in North America, where they had gone for post-graduate studies and were now settled in well-paying jobs and intending to remain for the foreseeable future. Her older son-in-law, now retired himself, was spending some of his time in Madras helping to look after her; periodically he would travel to Jeddah to be with his wife. Their youngest son, an engineering student at the Indian Institute of Technology, was the only one who remained behind in India. He had always been especially close to his grandmother. I clearly remember how, as a small boy, he would come home from school, rush immediately to Zakira Begum's room and beg her to tell him a story. He had hostel accommodations at the Institute but came home at least once or twice a week to see her. He did not want to leave her when his course was completed but he also had hopes—which have since been realized—of joining his siblings in the West for further study and better career opportunities than would be available in India.

All of Zakira Begum's family members were worried about her health and her emotional well-being, yet it was difficult for them either to leave their jobs and move back to India or to provide, from so many thousands of miles away, the kind of care and day-to-day companionship that they knew she needed at this time in her life. So they had been trying to persuade her to emigrate as well. There was no question of a permanent move to Saudi Arabia, since foreigners working there are required to return home once their term of employment has ended. But a Canadian visa might have been obtainable.

When I saw her last, the lengthy application process was in fact already underway. She had recently been taken for an interview with the medical panel appointed by the Canadian Consulate to assess the physical and mental condition of visa applicants. We laughed together as she told me how astonished the officials had been when she proved able to answer questions designed to test her mental acuity, such as the current day of the week and the name of India's Prime Minister! The next step in the process would be a physical exam. But she was not at all sure that she would go through with it. In fact, she admitted, she really didn't want to go overseas. Although she appreciated her offspring's legitimate concerns for her welfare, she was extremely reluctant to leave her home. In Diwan's Garden she had a large circle of close relatives and friends who kept an eye on her, dropping in to visit and chat with her on a daily basis and willingly running errands and doing whatever other tasks she needed help with. The daughters of her faithful, long-time cook and maid-of-all-work (a Hindu woman who had herself recently passed away) still came by every morning to prepare her meals, scrub the dishes and sweep the house. Her brother and sisters came from Hyderabad to spend extended periods with her, and her elder daughter, teaching in an Indian school in Saudi Arabia, often returned to Madras during school holidays to be with her. She wondered aloud what she would do with herself in a strange country whose language she had never fully mastered, whom she would talk to when her children and grandchildren were at work, how she would fill her time in the absence of the books and papers and the many unfinished writing projects that filled the shelves and piled up on chairs and on the floor of her room and still, despite her failing eyesight and her deteriorating health, continued to occupy her time and most of her energy.

Soon after my last visit, her elder daughter decided to return from Saudi Arabia for good and she and her husband were with Zakira Begum when she passed away the following year. In her final days her beloved younger grandson was continuously by her side. Though she is sorely missed by all of those who knew and loved her, it is perhaps just as well that in the end she was spared having to make the decision to leave the home in which she had spent most of her waking and sleeping hours for the past several decades of her life.

11

Thalaivar Amma
The Female Leader of Paiyur, Tamilnadu

SOUMHYA VENKATESAN

W hat is a portrait? You could think of it as a series of interactions each of which reveals or obscures aspects that are imperfectly or partially understood: a series of elicitations or concealments if you like. Word portraits emerge out of interactions between writer and subject—the outcome is the result of conversations, collaborations and spaces, proximities and distances. The following portrait is of a woman whom I have known for the past eight years. She lives in a small town in southern Tamilnadu, which I shall call Paiyur or the town of mats, hand-woven objects for which the town is famous in the Indian craft context.

* * *

1997: A whitewashed room in Paiyur's panchayat building. A woman sits at the desk. She is the Panchayat President. I ask if I can take a photograph of her. 'Wait,' she says, adjusting her sari so that the loose end thrown over one shoulder covers her head, and repositioning her chair so it is almost directly beneath a framed picture of Mohandas Karamchand Gandhi. 'Now you can take the photo.'

A few days later I am in her house. She is sitting in the yard, on the ground, in front of a wood-burning clay stove. On the stove is a deep terracotta pot filled with boiling liquid—the bubbles are a dark shade of purple. She lifts a bundle of split strands of *korai* into the pot and stirs briskly. Korai is a member of the sedge family of plants. Strands of dried and split *korai* stems form the weft of most mats woven in Tamilnadu. Around her are her daughters and grandchildren. One daughter is weaving on a mat loom, the others are chopping vegetables, preparing more *korai* for weaving, or just sitting and watching.

Meet Banu Beevi. In her mid-fifties, a Labbai Muslim, mat weaver and Panchayat President (1996–2000), she is articulate and active. As she works, she talks—about her political ambitions, becoming Panchayat President, weaving mats, the state of the nation and of the mat-weaving industry. She is given to using rich metaphors to illustrate the points she is making. Her daughters sometimes contradict her, at other times they remain silent and listen, or elaborate on things she has said. There are no men in the house even though she is married, as are two of her three daughters. Like most other men in Paiyur, they are migrant workers in the Middle East or they run small businesses elsewhere in India. The women rarely travel with or without their husbands, though Banu Beevi is an exception. Paiyur is 40 per cent Muslim. The Muslim population in the town is made up of Rauthers and Labbais—both Tamil Muslim subgroups. The Labbai Muslim group, from which the majority of the mat weavers for which the town is famed are drawn, is the smaller of the two, numbering around 650 people. The Labbais of Paiyur are not recent converts. Indeed Islam arrived on the southern coast of India very early on in the history of the religion, spreading inland through conversions and intermarriages. From the thirteenth century on waves of migrants from northern India brought more Muslim populations including the Rauthers, who derive their name from the Tamil word for horseman (*irauttar*), and who were Muslim horse troops. Considered a low-status group since colonial times, the traditional occupation of Labbais is said to be leading prayers at mosques and performing rituals for client households. The pay for such tasks is sporadic and irregular. Labbai and Rauther neighborhoods in Paiyur are more or less distinct. Intermarriage between the two groups is, according to most people, permitted though not common. People bring up this question of intermarriage to show that the divisions between Labbai and Rauther are not caste-like, rather they are based on the historical origins of the groups and irrelevant as far as marriage and commensality are concerned. The unity of the *jumma* or the Muslim congregation is a matter of pride and is often held up as a contrast to the divisiveness of the caste system in Hinduism. Nevertheless, it is generally agreed that Labbais are of lower status than Rauthers. A weaver, Wahab, told me that this was because Labbais acted as ritual specialists not just at marriages and other auspicious events but also at death ceremonies. Some Rauthers, he said, did not like to look at a Labbai first thing in the morning or before embarking on important work. The similarities with Hindu ideas of pollution are striking here. Recent reformist movements, which are beginning to gain popularity, and seeking to rid Islam of its syncretic practices, have also attacked the caste-like demarcations which exist between different kinds of Muslims.

Paiyur's Labbais do not own agricultural land, have few ties with the land and earn their livelihoods from the informal sectors of the economy. Several men migrate within and beyond India to earn money. The women live in Paiyur with their children, managing their households and earning some money through mat weaving, which they describe as their traditional occupation, or *beedi* or leaf cigarette rolling. Labbai women in Paiyur manage day-to-day household finances and make decisions relating to everyday matters, though more important decisions are made by men, often in consultation with the women.

It is common to see married Labbai women around town, taking their young children to school, carrying washing to the canal and frequenting the few shops, which mainly sell grocery and firewood. They also go to the mat shops and the cooperative society to sell their mats or collect payments. Sometimes one can see groups of women waiting to catch a bus to the nearest large town. Unmarried post-puberty girls are restricted to their homes and its immediate environs. Children of both sexes play in the streets and run in and out of various houses. One of the reasons that women give for their relative freedom of movement within the town is that everyone is a relative (*ellam sondakarar*). They also mention the same reason to explain why they do not move with their husbands to other places. One woman said, 'Here I can move around freely; we are all related. If I go to Bombay where my husband works, I cannot do that. I have to stay in the house. I get bored there.'

Banu Beevi, on the other hand, has travelled widely. When she was younger and her eldest two children were small, she was employed by the Tamilnadu state government to teach rural women in different parts of the state how to weave mats as part of income-generation schemes. This was when she met a Christian missionary whom she befriended and after whom her second daughter, Alice, is named. She has five children, three daughters and two sons; her younger son died in the year 2000.

Political and personal histories are closely intertwined. To identify oneself as a Muslim is not the same as to be identified as Muslim. This seems trivial, but is important. In December 1998, shortly before the anniversary of the demolition of the Babri Masjid, and partly because the body of a man who was a member of the Tamil Munnani, a right-wing Hindu organization, was found near the Muslim area in Paiyur, many young Muslim men were arrested by the police on 'precautionary grounds'. Banu Beevi's son was one of them even though his family and others in Paiyur say he was never involved in politics. He did not spend a long time in jail, but fell ill shortly after his release and never recovered, though the family tried everything they could to help him. After all, he was their hope: they had saved and scraped to ensure that he had received a good education. The family had hoped that he would get a job in the formal sector of the economy which would help his parents and siblings considerably. The family was shattered by his death. His going to jail had been bad enough. 'Who will give him a job now? Who will let him marry their daughter?' his mother had said bitterly. But now that he was dead, those seemed like small concerns. 'We dressed him up like a bridegroom for his funeral', one of his sisters told me. 'He died before he could get married.' The ceremony on the 40th day after his death was a muted, though lavish, event. I was in town, but not invited. 'He must have caught the brain fever that killed him in jail. Why must they take our boys?'

Banu Beevi's daughters were all educated in the local school until they attained puberty. They were then withdrawn from school to stay at home until they would be married. This is common among the Muslims of Paiyur. However, Banu Beevi says that she would have let her youngest daughter continue going to school had it not been for the murder and the subsequent troubles. 'Some of our boys did cause problems', 'but not all of them', she said. 'But I still did not want to send my daughter to the school in Paiyur. We thought of sending her to school in the nearby town, but that was too difficult for several reasons.' The daughter, Saira, now stays at home and weaves mats and performs other household chores. When we last met, Banu Beevi was arranging her marriage, though that can only take place once the family has got some money. Dowry demands are high in Paiyur and the bride's family is responsible for the entire expense of the marriage.

It is difficult to know if Banu Beevi and her husband Kareemullah would really have let Saira continue with her education. Few Muslims in Paiyur do, and though Banu Beevi is unusually outgoing, there are still many things in which she conforms to larger social norms. This includes the ways in which she has brought up her daughters. Some Muslim girls in the neighboring town (which several people in Paiyur describe as more strict in Islamic practice) continue with their schooling even after puberty; veiled or with their heads covered some even go on to tertiary education.

In Paiyur however, few Labbai girls or women wear the veil, only covering their heads when the call to prayer from the mosque is heard across the town, or when they are praying themselves. One woman told me that wearing the *burqa* or full veil was only for rich women. 'You need to have good clothes and jewellery to show respect to the *burqa*. We are not decent enough.' Further conversation revealed that she was making the point that women who needed to earn their living could not adopt constricting or restraining clothing like the full veil. Rather they did what they needed to do, at the same time trying to be modest.

Post-puberty girls and young unmarried women thus earn money by rolling *beedi*s at home or weaving, they also learn to recite parts of the Quran and help with the cooking. Their fathers, brothers, mothers or married sisters bring them the necessary tools, raw materials and other things they require. Men, and more rarely married women, go shopping for clothes for festive occasions.

Unlike some other Muslim families I know in Paiyur, neither Banu Beevi nor her daughters discuss religious practice in much detail (or at least not in my presence). Some of Banu Beevi's granddaughters and one daughter fasted during one Ramzan when I was there, others do not and there is not much discussion about this, though the eldest daughter Jannat told me that, having to look after her children and weave to feed them, it was difficult for her to observe the fast.

All three of Banu Beevi's daughters learned how to weave mats after their menarche. Banu Beevi herself only learned to weave the high-quality mats of Paiyur after her marriage when she moved to Paiyur where her husband was based. I know little about her childhood or earlier life apart from the fact that it was not unusual, and like most Labbai women in the town she was married to a kinsman; she is also related in multiple ways to other Paiyur Labbais. Mat weaving has stood her in good stead, allowing her to earn an income when money from her husband (who does not have a job) is scarce. Even though he can weave and is generally acknowledged as one of the best weavers in town, Banu Beevi's husband is more often than not away trying to earn money from Tamil Muslim settlers in Southeast Asia. He is said to be very skilled at fortune telling, and at dispensing 'country medicines' and his services are in brisk demand wherever he goes. Unfortunately for the household, he is also fond of gambling and sends little money home. The eldest son has disappeared—no one knows where he is. This makes life hard for Jannat, the eldest daughter, as she is married to the brother of her brother's wife. Such exchange marriages, where a household gives a girl and accepts one in return, are common. They are popular because they allow families to share the expenses of marriages and keep dowry and other demands from escalating.

'People call me *thalaivar amma* (mother/female leader)', Banu Beevi says this often and with pride. 'Everyone wants me to come and bless their newborn babies, inaugurate new ventures or just visit them.' Her daughters sometimes smile, sometimes look grim-faced; they know what this popularity has cost them.

The year that Banu Beevi ran for the post of Panchayat President, the seat was reserved for a female candidate. She stood for election as an independent candidate against women from Tamilnadu's two largest political parties—the Dravida Munnetra Kazhagam (DMK) and the All India Anna Dravida Munnetra Kazhagam (AIADMK). When she won, she says, there was much surprise. How could she, a Labbai Muslim woman with no party affiliation have beaten women backed by a lot of money and political resources? 'I spent Rs 17,000 [on another occasion she told me she had spent Rs 100,000]. Everyone was fed up with the political parties and the way they always lie and play off groups against each other. The Muslims voted for me even though one of the other candidates was also Muslim.'

A young Muslim man, Raja, who was also a panchayat member, said to me, 'we voted for her because we thought she would be able to make money and we could all get some. But she has not been able to make much, so it has not been very good for us. We will not vote for her again. Women do not know how to make money.'

Banu Beevi is seemingly oblivious to this criticism. Indeed, at the end of her four-year term, she wanted to contest the elections again and did so despite her daughters' protests. They felt that it would cost money that they could ill-afford. Banu Beevi lost the election. Part of the reason for her loss may be that the seat was now open to men and women—no other woman contested the election. The monetary fall-out from this, and from the bail money they had to raise to get their son out of jail, as well as the money spent on medical expenses for him still affect the entire family.

Family is important for the rural poor, and this is not just because of the bonds of affection, birth and marriage that hold people together. There are no financial safety nets, and few hopes of money from the formal sectors of the economy for them. When troubles come, as they often do, or events such as marriages, it is from family that money can be expected—this does have to be reciprocated, but there is often a time lag which provides some breathing space. Moneylenders and informal community-specific local rolling credit schemes (chit fund schemes) are also accessed to raise money. Needless to say, with moneylenders the rates of interest are extremely high—3–5 per cent per month.

Banu Beevi's eldest daughter Jannat's husband is in the Middle East. He has been there ever since my first visit to Paiyur in 1996, though, according to Jannat, neither of them is happy about this. But they had no choice. 'He is in the desert tending goats, no one for company. Once a week his employer drives over with supplies. He sees no one. He was there and came back saying he would never go again, and now we have this money trouble. I have had to send him back to that hell. We have no choice. We also have many daughters.' For someone who has lived in Paiyur, with its cheek-by-jowl housing, open doors, and the knowledge that everyone is kin, isolation in the desert with only goats to provide company must be particularly difficult to bear.

There are many facets to Banu Beevi's character, but one thing that strikes me, as an anthropologist, is her ambition, her desire to make a mark in the world. There are far more avenues for men to shine in the public sphere, yet Banu Beevi has managed to do precisely that both through her panchayat position and within the mat-weaving industry. The latter was a struggle; influence had hitherto been restricted to office-bearers of the mat-weaving cooperative society (or the Society as people in the town call it) and private mat traders who are also Labbais, though males. This only changed when a non-governmental organization (NGO), Craft Enterprises, started work in Paiyur in 1995. Craft Enterprises sought to revive and develop the mat-weaving industry both through 'building capabilities' and by establishing a steady market for the mats in Indian cities.

Even though Craft Enterprises initially worked with private traders, it was soon approached by weavers who requested the NGO to buy mats directly from them. Banu Beevi described her reasons for this in 1997: 'The private traders give advances and loans and then we have to keep selling them mats to repay them. Even when you do not owe them any money, they take a long time to pay for your mats and you cannot take new mats to someone else, as they will delay their payments even more. They cast their nets and trap us like fish. We cannot escape.'

Ten weaving households worked closely with Craft Enterprises. Within this group Banu Beevi was acknowledged as a leader and referred to as *thalaivar amma*. Her active role in the NGO to a certain extent coincided with her panchayat presidency—this is not surprising. There is, as in many other parts of the country, a great respect for people in official positions. She was initially president of the Craft Enterprises group, signing every cheque that was made out to weavers and holding joint control over the group's bank account in Paiyur. Over time her influence waned as other weavers sought to acquire more active roles for themselves and as she herself sought to make her mark on the mat-weaving industry through other means, one of which involved trying to get a National Award.

The National Award scheme for excellence in craft practice was initiated by the central government in 1965. Kamaladevi Chattopadhyay, the founder president of the Handicrafts Board, the apex body for craft development in India saw it as a way of extending patronage to craft production which had suffered under colonial rule. Every year around 1,500 craft objects are submitted to the awards competition by craft producers, NGOs or state agencies. While on the face of it the selection committee chooses award winners on the basis of the objects submitted, in practice, other considerations are important. The award winner should also be a social leader who has made a positive contribution to the craft as a whole. Furthermore, special consideration would be given to 'languishing crafts'. Within Paiyur, weavers seem most concerned with what the award will do for them—the cash prize is attractive, as is the visibility in the media and within the craft development mechanism that awards bring, but equally, if not more so, is the perception of award winners as 'having ears in high places'. Awards therefore make visible people's influence and their presence in national networks.

The first national award winner in Paiyur was a woman whose father, Mohammad, like Banu Beevi, was also considered a local *thalaivar* or leader. This award, made in 1992, continues to be controversial in some circles. Banu Beevi and her husband are insistent that the award-winning mat was, in fact, partly made by Banu Beevi's husband, and that the only reason the award was given, was the influence that Mohammad was able to wield in bureaucratic circles in Delhi through his relationship with influential brahmans in Paiyur.

Banu Beevi is extremely anxious to win a national award. There are many reasons why this is important to her, one of which is that it will reinforce her claim that she and her husband are among the most skilled mat weavers in Paiyur. The award will also make visible her influence within the craft worlds, which comprise, along with makers, government officials, development agents and other urban élites interested in craft. This seems important to her in the same way that being Panchayat President did at one time, being a way of extending her sphere of influence and entering into larger open networks than are possible for a Labbai female.

Between 1997 and 2004, Banu Beevi wove two mats for submissions to the national awards competitions. Both the mats were elaborate productions— one had a picture of a peacock picked out in colored silk threads and the other had a portrait of a famous early Tamil poet philosopher woven into it in *korai*. The latter used natural dyes. Each of these mats took a month to weave. Their manufacture required a significant expenditure of time and money and in opportunity cost—neither was sponsored by any organization, and so the cost of materials and time spent all devolved on Banu Beevi and her household. The mats also necessitated several trips by Banu Beevi to the local handicrafts board office in a neighboring town as the mat needed to be certified as Banu Beevi's work. Both she and her husband made a trip to Madras to hand in the second mat at the Tamilnadu state craft development office. They also used this visit to meet some important craft developers in Madras to seek support for their entry. The first mat that she submitted did not win an award.[1] This, though a blow to her, was not unexpected. Two mats from Paiyur had already won awards in the 1990s—the mat-weaving industry had therefore already received significant support from the state and was unlikely to receive more support in the form of new awards. Additionally, both the mats that won awards conformed in their color scheme and patterns to the aesthetic model considered appropriate and authentic for craft mats. That is to say they had geometric patterns and, in the case of the second award-winning mat, used natural dyes, something that the state and non-governmental sector have been seeking to encourage. Indeed the patterns of both award-winning mats were specified by craft developers.

Banu Beevi was more ambitious in her choice of design—choosing to make mats that showcased both her technical skill, and reflected her own

---

[1] I heard through someone else that the second mat did win an award (2006), though I have not been able to confirm this.

aesthetic sensibilities. She also sought to make explicit the ideological link between craft and nation, something that has become important since the early twentieth century, by choosing to weave symbols of the nation on her mats. The peacock is India's national bird, and the poet Thiruvalluvar an extremely important regional and national figure.

Both mats reveal, to my mind, Banu Beevi's creative engagement with the craft development mechanism, and her attempts to make her mark in the wider world by working within that context. At the same time she is intensely aware of some of the contradictions that might come into play when a Muslim weaver is identified as a traditional Indian craft producer. Her discussion with a prominent craft developer, Somnath, is telling in this regard.

During a visit to Paiyur in 2002, Somnath discussed with Banu Beevi his idea that craft producers, rather than being anonymous as has been customary, should start signing their objects as artists do. This, he felt would both add more value to craft objects and enhance the status of the makers. Banu Beevi strongly disagreed. The mats made in Paiyur are increasingly commonly bought for Hindu ritual use—this along with the craft market, constitutes the weavers' main market. People, she felt, might be reluctant about buying objects made by Muslims for ritual use or even for other purposes. In the current climate, it is better to be a bit discreet especially when one does not know who will come into contact with the mats and through them with the makers.

There are however, other times when Banu Beevi is happy for her name to be associated with the mats and with particular kinds of projects. When I commissioned mats from Paiyur for an exhibition at a museum,[2] several weavers participated in the project. The mats for the museum, as several people in Paiyur were quick to realize, would be lasting testimonies of their skill, seen by many people and therefore also a way to publicize the mat-weaving industry. Banu Beevi wove a mat on which she not only wove her name but also that of Craft Enterprises. For her, this mat was a way of making herself as well as her allegiance to the NGO visible.

But at the same time, Banu Beevi was also working with the mat weavers' cooperative society in Paiyur, which is hostile to Craft Enterprises, and in 1999 sought to eject from its membership those weavers who worked with the NGO. This is in accordance with her philosophy and indeed with that of several people in Paiyur; they feel they have few choices and are therefore

---

[2] The Museum of Archaeology and Anthropology, Cambridge University.

unwilling to alienate any institution that may be of some help to them. When she was Panchayat President for example, she worked closely with the head of the regional government to have money sanctioned for a new weaving shed in the cooperative society's compound. This was partly a political move for which both Banu Beevi and the local District Commissioner were keen to take credit. The sanctioning of the money and the shed itself embodied their efficaciousness.

As subsequent events showed, Banu Beevi was right not to alienate the cooperative society and private traders in Paiyur. Craft Enterprises suddenly had its funding pulled out in late 2001 and all the weavers who were associated with it had to make their peace with either the private traders or with the cooperative society if they wanted to continue weaving. Banu Beevi started weaving for one of the private traders in Paiyur after accepting his condition that she should not supply mats to any other trader or NGO. This was when she embarked on her second attempt in 2003–04 to win a national award (discussed earlier). In part this seemed to be a way of breaking away from the control of the trader and acquiring the kind of legitimacy in the craft worlds that a national award confers. But as I discussed earlier, it was also a way of showing that she had influence with craft élites.

At the same time Banu Beevi was also exploring other avenues. In late 2003, she accompanied her husband on one of his trips to Southeast Asia where she sought to help him earn some money. The favorable exchange rate means that even a small amount earned in Singapore or Malaysia translates to a large sum of money in Indian rupees. In order to make this trip, Banu Beevi had to borrow money for the air tickets and the visa. She also had to leave her youngest unmarried daughter alone in the house, and relied on her older daughters to sleep over and generally provide company and chaperonage. Again in this matter, Banu Beevi was blazing a new path, one that was the subject of much discussion in Paiyur. The close proximity of Labbai houses and the fact that every Labbai is considered kin means that people are aware of each others' movements and discuss them extensively. At the time when Banu Beevi was away to Southeast Asia, most people I spoke to in Paiyur were critical of her decision to travel, albeit interested in her experience. One woman said, 'she has gone and if it works out, then perhaps I will go too.'

Money was extremely tight in the household when Banu Beevi was away. It was the month of Ramzan and her daughters were trying to weave as much as they could in order to sell their mats and earn money. Buying new clothes for Eid at the end of Ramzan was out of the question. Yet, on the afternoon of Eid when I turned up in the house, all three daughters were wearing new sarees in shiny polyester. Banu Beevi had managed at the last minute to send lengths of cloth through someone who was coming to Paiyur. She and her husband had been given these by the owner of a cloth warehouse for whom they had performed a service.

✻ ✻ ✻

When one returns after a long time, people in Paiyur say: 'my eyes were searching for you'. As an anthropologist who has spent significant periods of time there since 1996, my eyes too search for things that provide a larger context, a better way for understanding the choices that the Labbai Muslims of Paiyur make. In that sense the whole world potentially becomes a backdrop for the people I work with and care about. The day war was declared on Iraq in 2003, for example, I was in Paiyur watching some men packing to leave for Kuwait. They had borrowed money to pay a travel agent for visas and air tickets the previous year and these had just come through. They could not afford to cancel the trip despite misgivings. Earlier the anti-Muslim riots in Bombay in 1994 had meant that many men who lived and worked in that city left their jobs and returned to Paiyur in fear of their lives. Though a small town in the southernmost part of Tamilnadu, Paiyur is caught up in global and national events. In these situations it is important to know what to say when, and how to moderate one's behavior, self-presentations and representations. As Banu Beevi discovered one day to her shock: as Panchayat President she was attending a meeting wearing an orange saree with a lotus flower border. A few people came up to her, she said, and asked her why as a Muslim she was wearing the colors of the Bharatiya Janata Party—the political party in power at the time known for its Hindu nationalist agenda. Even colors and flowers are dangerous, she said, and we have to think all the time about what we look like, say, and do. Even if one does not want it, the world comes to one.

It is difficult to write about a person. What I know about Banu Beevi comes not only from my interactions with her, but also from conversations with her daughters and with others in Paiyur. It also comes from a wider awareness of what is going on locally, regionally, nationally and internationally. Perhaps it is I who puts these things together to create a composite picture of a person in a particular time and place. An art-historian friend, Tom de Wesselow, was once talking about what dark sections do in paintings. Some parts of the composition are light and immediately visible, but there are other bits in the background that gradually emerge as you spend more time looking at the painting. These change the way you see the painting, making it more complex and altering your perceptions of what is going on. At first sight, one sees Banu Beevi as an unusual and strong Muslim woman who has achieved something that few other women have in this small Indian town. It is only slowly, as one gets to know the place and its people, that the full extent of how much she has done and how much more she wants become somewhat comprehensible, as do the various constraints within which she operates. The background keeps expanding—Paiyur becomes bigger, actions and attitudes very far away impact on individual lives, they change the choices available to individuals like Banu Beevi. She then becomes both a product of history, and one who seeks to shape it through the various means available to her.

Notes on Contributors

MANUELA CIOTTI is Research Associate, Centre for South Asian Studies, University of Edinburgh.

LAWRENCE COHEN is Associate Professor, University of California, Berkeley.

BRIAN J. DIDIER is Andrew W. Mellon Postdoctoral Fellow in Anthropology and Religion, Dartmouth College.

THOMAS BLOM HANSEN is Professor of Religious Studies at the Faculty of Social and Behavioural Sciences, Universiteit van Amsterdam.

FARHANA IBRAHIM is Visiting Fellow, Department of Sociology, National University of Singapore.

CRAIG JEFFREY is Associate Professor in Geography and International Studies, University of Washington.

PATRICIA JEFFERY is Professor of Sociology, School of Social and Political Sciences, University of Edinburgh.

ROGER JEFFERY is Professor of the Sociology of South Asia, School of Social and Political Sciences, University of Edinburgh.

SHAIL MAYARAM is Senior Fellow, Centre for the Study of Developing Societies, New Delhi.

APARNA RAO was affiliated as Research Scholar with the Centre for the Study of Developing Societies in Delhi between 2003 and 2004. In June 2005, she was appointed Directeur de Recherche at the École des Hautes Études (EHES) in Paris. She passed away on 28 June 2005.

EDWARD SIMPSON is Lecturer in Social Anthropology, School of Oriental and African Studies, London.

SYLVIA VATUK is Professor Emerita, Department of Anthropology, University of Illinois at Chicago.

SOUMHYA VENKATESAN is Lecturer in Social Anthropology at the University of Manchester.